Perfect Phrases for Business Letters

Hundreds of Ready-to-Use Phrases
for Writing Effective Business Letters,
Memos, E-Mail, and More

Ken O'Quinn

McGraw-Hill

New York Chicago San Francisco Lisbon
London Madrid Mexico City Milan New Delhi
San Juan Seoul Singapore Sydney Toronto

The **McGraw·Hill** *Companies*

1 2 3 4 5 6 7 8 9 0   FGR/FGR 0 9 8 7 6 5

ISBN 0-07-145976-6

This book is printed on recycled, acid-free paper containing a minimum of 50% recycled, de-inked fiber.

McGraw-Hill books are available at special quantity discounts to use as premiums and sales promotions, or for use in corporate training programs. For more information, please write to the Director of Special Sales, Professional Publishing, McGraw-Hill, Two Penn Plaza, New York, NY 10121-2298. Or contact your local bookstore.

Perfect Phrases for Business Letters

To Lori
Ben, Hillary, Jaime, and Pat

Acknowledgments

Numerous people played a role, directly or indirectly, in the writing of this book, and I appreciate their support. A special thanks to Don Murray, an award-winning writer, author, and coach who encouraged me to write a book and the person from whom I have learned the most about writing; to Don Ferguson, at Fleishman Hillard, for his insight and support; to Wayne Cowart and Dana McDaniel, linguists at the University of Southern Maine, whose simplified, detailed explanations of how language works have been invaluable; and to Terry and Leigh Bagley, who loaned me a typewriter to start my consulting business in 1993.

Table of Contents

Chapter 3: Specific Types of Business Letters 45

Chapter 4: Memos   89

Chapter 5: News Releases   115

Part One

Getting Started Writing Business Letters

Part One

Chapter 1

Organizing Your Message

Perhaps you find that the most difficult first step in writing is not giving birth to the first sentence but garnering the necessary discipline to sit down and commit yourself to the blank screen. You avoid as long as you can: You think of other things you need to do and pretend that they are more important, you go get another cup of coffee, you stick your head in a friend's office and chat, or you clean your desk and promise to get to the writing task tomorrow.

This powerful force that seeks to distract us from writing and to kill our creativity and spirit is called resistance. It is a more difficult habit to break than drugs or liquor, says author Stephen Pressfield. Resistance is the enemy within.[1]

Recognizing resistance for what it is will enable you to ask why it is occurring. Are you worried about the reader's response? Is your manager's critical editing voice resonating in your mind? Is something unrelated to the writing task weighing on your mind?

Perhaps you lack confidence, which sometimes is self-inflicted. Writers, like athletes, often hamper their performance with what is called negative self-talk. An athlete leaves the field mumbling, "I can't afford to make such stupid mistakes." Similarly when you say, "I can't write," it is self-defeating, and you avoid accepting responsibility for what it is: a choice. As psychiatrists frequently tell drug addicts and alcoholics, we all make choices. The problem is not that you "can't"; it is that you choose not to.

So avoid such negative words as *can't, should, must,* and *have to.* They are counterproductive. Instead, inject a positive tone by converting those words to *want, wish, desire, choose,* and *prefer.*[2]

When we say, "I *should* have written," "I *must* develop," and "I *have to* make this impressive," we impose pressure on ourselves and we feel guilty and incompetent for failing to achieve what might be an unreasonable standard. It is better to say, "I *can* develop a strong proposal," or "I *want* to make this impressive."

Once the adrenalin is flowing and you are ready to start, you need to unscramble the array of thoughts swirling in your head so that you can create an orderly structure and have a sense of where you are going. Writing is similar to building a house. Imagine if you hired carpenters to build you a new home and they showed up the first day and began building with no blueprints. "No problem," they tell you. "We'll figure it out as we go along." You probably will not want to live in the house.

Similarly, you cannot effectively write a communication of significance by thinking it through as you go. You might contend that you do not have time to organize your thoughts before starting, but when you reach the sixth or seventh paragraph and realize how haphazard the writing is, you will consume a significant chunk of time revising and rearranging the material to make it coherent. Some of that time you could save by investing more effort in mapping your ideas before you start.

A two- or three-sentence e-mail might not require extensive forethought, but many other messages do. Any substantive message, one that contains hard information pertaining to daily business activities or operations, deserves careful attention.

Don Murray, a Pulitzer Prize–winning writer and a nationally known author and writing coach, introduced the concept of writing as a four-step process: planning, drafting, revising, and editing. Critical work is done in the planning phase, before you put down your first word. This is when you unscramble your mind, sort out your ideas, and establish a sense of direction. By starting to write before you truly know what you want to say, you will wander, putting down ideas in the random order in which they occur to you. Most readers will not have the patience to drift along with you because you will not appear to be in control of the writing.

Brainstorming

To establish a road map so that you write coherently, try brainstorming on paper, an exercise in which you randomly jot down words, phrases, or ideas relating to the topics you want to cover. Unloading your mind enables you to display your raw material in front of you and to answer the questions, "What do I want to include?" and "In what order do I want to present the information?"

As you write ideas, you will think of new ones as a result of free association, a brainstorming technique that author Tony Buzan calls "radiant thinking."[3] Draw a circle on a piece of paper, and inside the circle, put your purpose in writing the document. Then draw lines branching out from the circle, the way first-grade children draw the sun. On each branch, list a topic that you will want to discuss in the message, and if that prompts you to think of a related word or idea, add it on a branch off of the original word. See Figure 1.1.

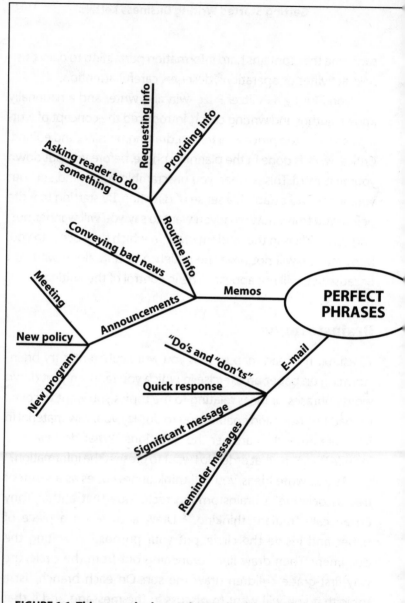

FIGURE 1.1 This example shows what my brainstorming looked like as I began to contemplate what to include in this book. This exercise invites you to expand your array of topics by way of free association.

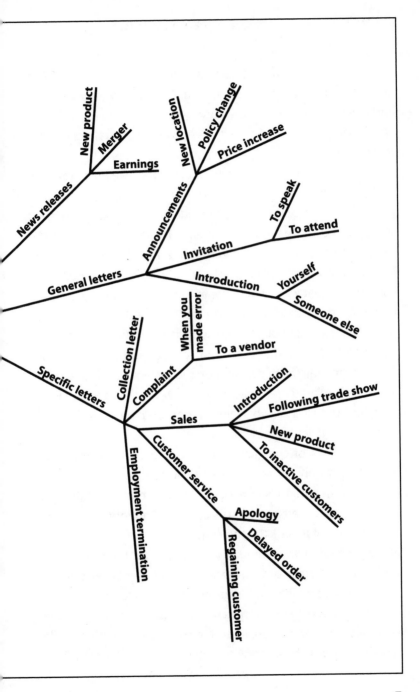

The advantage to this approach over a simple list is that it lends itself to spontaneous thinking. As you explore your mind and write down topics, those words will trigger new associations, which you can add on a new branch, and the diagram continues to expand.

An alternative to the broader, more expansive brainstorming design is a list (see Figure 1.2). This could be simply a vertical presentation of topics, with related ideas appearing as indented subtopics under main subject areas. Or the list could take the form of a traditional outline with Roman numerals and related ideas appearing as *A, B, C,* etc. The disadvantage to listing, Buzan contends, is that when you write in a linear manner, the moment you write the last letter of the topic or key word, you unconsciously sense that you are finished with that thought. You then move on and try to think of a new topic to add to your list, preventing the brain from dwelling on the previous topic and thinking of new, related ideas. Nevertheless, when the message is not long and detailed or when you are hurried, listing your topics might be sufficient to get you started.

Regardless of the design you use to brainstorm, let the ideas flow freely. Write down any topics that come to mind, even ideas that might seem foolish. Do not stop to edit the list as you proceed, because it will disrupt your thought process, and do not attempt to rank the topics in an order before you have finished unloading your mind. If you have eight topics to discuss and you put them in order after you have written down only four, it will be more difficult to insert the remaining topics.

After you have written down the ideas, determine which ones are important (circle or highlight them with a yellow marker), see which ones link to others and where there is dupli-

RANDOM ORDER	RANKED BY SEQUENCE OR IMPORTANCE
	1. ___topic___
Letters	2. ___topic___
Specific letters	3. ___topic___

Letters

Specific letters
- complaint
- sales
  introduction
  follow-up
  new product
  to regain inactive customers
- collection letter
- termination

General letters
- introductory
- invitations
  to speak
  to attend
- announcements
  policy changes
  price increases
  move to new location

Memos

Routine
- requesting information
- providing information
- asking reader to do something

Conveying bad news
- criticism
- reprimand
- rejection

FIGURE 1.2 This example shows what ideas look like when presented in a vertical list. Although mapping lends itself to more elaborate thinking, simply listing topics and then putting them in the order in which you want to present them might be adequate for short writing or speaking tasks or for when you are hurried.

cation, and decide which topics are no longer important enough to include. You will quickly notice what you forgot to mention because the topic is conspicuously absent from your array of ideas.

Choosing a Format

How you arrange your topics will depend on the format that is appropriate for the message. Not all communication calls for the same organizational structure. Do you want to proceed from most to least important (the most common pattern), in an indirect order (bad news), in a problem-solution format, or in a sequential order? Number your topics according to when you want to discuss that subject (first? second? third?) in whatever format you choose.

Consider the Reader

Planning your writing means more than simply determining what you want to say; you also need to consider whom you will say it to. Affecting what you put in will be such things as what the reader wants to know and what additional factors might influence how the reader interprets the information.

"Know your audience" might be the oldest principle of communication, yet it is one that is commonly forgotten. Whether or not a reader remains engaged in the message and grasps your intended meaning often depends on whether you have taken certain issues into consideration.

Here are four questions that you should always ask before sending a message:

Getting Started Writing Business Letters

1. What are the essential points that the reader needs to know?
2. What information does the reader want to know? This is not the same as the first question. Beyond what is most important for the reader to know is information that you know the reader will be looking for. Do not force the reader to make phone calls and write e-mail notes in search of those details.
3. What do I want the reader to do? Not every message will contain a request or issue a directive, but if there is an action you want the reader to take, be sure to position it near the beginning.
4. What is the deadline? Far too many messages include a deadline in the last paragraph, and it usually is appropriate and more effective to put it in the first few sentences.

In addition, here are other important questions. Not all of them will apply to every message, but at least consider them.

1. **Will the reader immediately understand the content?** Just because someone is in the same industry or even in the same department is no assurance that he or she will immediately comprehend your message. Perhaps it has been days since you last discussed the topic, and a significant amount of information about other issues has crossed the person's desk in that time. Or maybe your word choice and sentence structure will leave the reader uncertain about your meaning.
2. **How will the reader react?** Will the reader be worried, annoyed, confused, angry, or embarrassed? Will the reader feel inconvenienced? If so, maybe some additional explanation or a tweaking of the wording might make it

easier for the person to accept your request, or it might reduce the likelihood that the reader will misinterpret your meaning.

3. **How interested is the reader in this topic?** A topic might be of great importance to you but is only of casual interest to the reader. If that is the case, writing an exhaustive message will only discourage the reader from giving it much attention. Even if the person does take the time to read it, your significant points could become smothered under all the information you include.

4. **Who else is likely to read this, and will that person understand the content?** Many messages are read by more than the intended receiver because other people need to see it. The reader will pass it on for someone else's reaction or approval. If you think about the additional readers, it will help to ensure that you include sufficient information for them to make any needed decisions.

Organization

Organizing—thinking about your topics, the audience, and additional factors—ensures that you present your information to the reader in a sequence that not only is logical but is most effective for the given information, and that reduces the time the reader needs to process it. A written message, like a speech, is easier to follow when points are made in an order. Arranging thoughts also ensures that your key points are presented in the right locations for emphasis or for strategic reasons.

A failure to organize has risks. The message is more likely to be unfocused, with important points sprinkled randomly throughout the page. The reader might miss the main point or might misinterpret the importance of the message. If the message is vague or confusing because the thoughts are not coherently developed, the reader also will likely leave.

If, after organizing, you struggle to get the first sentence written, perhaps you need to relax. People often become tense when they begin to put words to paper, because they are concerned about making it flawless. Only after you have made numerous revisions to improve it will you submit it as a draft. The initial version is for your eyes only, so put your mind at ease and let the words flow. Following the road map you created while brainstorming, you need to transfer your ideas to the screen without interruption.

That means you cannot stop to edit while you are writing, or you will lose track of your thought. Reaching for a dictionary or thesaurus is a great idea when the time is right, but now is not the time. Insert a capital *X* where you need to put a word and continue on; you can search for that word after you have finished, when you are revising.

Two sides of the brain are working when you write, the creative right side and the critical left side. The right side, dominant in artists and poets, is strong in imagination and creativity. It is the side that wants to express your fresh ideas. The left side, which is influential in activities that require significant use of language and math, is more logical, analytical, and structural. The left side contains the critical voice you hear second-guessing your decisions about organization, content, word choice, and sentence structure.

To allow your creativity to flourish, you need to suppress the critical voice that impedes your progress. The time to listen to it is later. Separate the writing and editing stages so that you benefit from each one independently. First, ease your standards and be tolerant as you write rapidly in the drafting phase. The time to be a tough editor is when you are in the revising stage, trimming excess information, moving pieces around, and shaping the material into a piece of writing that satisfies you.

The editing phase is reserved for touch-ups and final tweaking. Line-by-line proofreading for grammar, punctuation, and stylebook errors should be left until the final step of the editing stage.

Throughout the writing process, from the moment you try to start until the final draft is complete, work with colleagues whose editing advice you trust. People often avoid asking co-workers questions about writing, and they often will not ask anyone to read their draft, because they do not want to reveal what they do not know. By not making themselves vulnerable, they lose a tremendous opportunity to learn from others. Most business professionals struggle with similar issues when it comes to writing; no one should be embarrassed.

What You Will Find in the Book

The book will serve as a useful resource to everyone from administrative assistants to senior executives who write letters, memos, e-mail, short reports, and other forms of business communication. It provides how-to suggestions, and it invites people to view writing as more than merely putting information on the screen and hitting the *send* button.

People write messages in many different workplace situations, requiring that they decide how to begin, what to include, what to remove, how to end, and what kind of tone to use. The book offers tips and techniques for getting started and for writing clear, efficient, compelling prose, and it includes hundreds of suggested phrases that can jump-start a writing task when you know what you want to say but struggle to find the right words.

References

[1] Stephen Pressfield, *The War of Art* (New York: Warner Books, 2002), p. 8.

[2] Dorothy Corkille Briggs, *Celebrate Your Self* (New York: Broadway Books, 1977), p. 52.

[3] Tony Buzan, *The Mind Map Book* (New York: Penguin Books, 1993), p. 57.

Part Two

Perfect Phrases for Business Letters

Chapter 2

General Business Letters

The Value of a Letter

The Internet has brought new tools for communicating quickly, such as e-mail, instant messaging, and text messaging, but a carefully written letter still has its place. A letter on company letterhead or personal stationery gives the impression that care and effort went into writing the letter, making it more meaningful than many hastily written e-mail messages.

Letters can be more efficient and effective than telephone calls and e-mail. Given the pace of today's workplace, people often forget voice-mail messages and electronic notes, and information can be too detailed or too complicated to be absorbed quickly on the phone.

When crafting a letter, keep in mind a few key elements. It must be clear, efficient, complete, and professionally conversational. Use common, plain words so that the reader can breeze through the writing; remove any information that is not pertinent to the main point(s) of the letter; be sure all the reader's questions are answered; and have a courteous, friendly tone that resembles the kind of face-to-face conversation you would have with a customer.

Avoid the common mistake of taking too long to say why you are writing. Too many letters back in to the primary point of the message, which wastes the reader's time and also increases the likelihood that the reader will miss the point or will misinterpret it. In most letters, the reader should know within the first two sentences why he or she is being asked to read this.

Salutations

- Dear Mr. Jones,
- Dear Ms. Jones, (if you do not know whether the person prefers Mrs. or Miss)
- Dear Pat Martin, (when you do not know the reader's gender)
- Dear Jack, (when you know the person or if you are comfortable on a first-name basis)
- Hi Pam/Pam, (a letter or e-mail to someone you know)
- Dear Senator Collins,/Governor Ballam,
- Dear Reverend Smith,/Commissioner Samson,/Chief Thompson,/ Colonel Krans,
- Dear Dr. Reynolds,
- Dear Accounting Staff, (when you do not know the exact person to contact)
- Dear Client Services Representative,

Tips

- Do not abbreviate titles in the greeting.
- Spell all names and titles correctly.
- "Dear Sir or Madam" and "To whom it may concern" are no longer acceptable.
- A colon or a comma can be used after the name, but a comma is softer and friendlier.

Transitions

- Inside this proposal
- Plus, you will receive
- That's not all. You also will
- Another issue is
- Because of these circumstances,
- In addition to those changes, we also
- Such issues present us with a challenge
- *That* recommendation raises a few issues (Use a pronoun to refer back.)
- This is important to us for several reasons.
- Let me clarify.
- One final consideration
- However, consequently, nevertheless, conversely, on the other hand (transitional expressions that express a contrast to something said previously)
- Furthermore, also, similarly, in addition, equally significant (transitional expressions that suggest you are adding thoughts or linking related information)
- That is why, as a result, therefore, for that reason, given that (transitional expressions that convey purpose or consequence)

Tips

- Transitions help to build coherence in writing by showing the reader the relationship between ideas. That enables the reader to move fluidly through the information.
- When transition words and phrases appear at the start of the sentence, they often (though not always) are followed by a comma.

➡

- Be sure to choose the appropriate transition. Notice that the sentence "Not everyone can attend, and we will meet anyway" is awkward because *and* gives equal importance to both ideas. *But* or *however*, which denote a contrast, would be appropriate.
- If you are confused as to whether a word or phrase is a transitional expression or some other part of speech, remember that transitional expressions can always be shifted to another place in the sentence without changing the meaning.

Closings

Formal

- Sincerely
- Cordially
- Respectfully yours
- Very truly yours
- Respectfully

Professional but Warmer

- Regards
- Kind regards
- With warm regards
- Yours truly

Friendly Closing

- Best wishes
- Warmest wishes
- All the best
- Thanks for your help

Tips

- Among the most common closings are *sincerely* and *kind regards*. They fit all occasions.
- The closing should reflect the nature of the message, your relationship with the reader, and your personality.

Introducing Yourself

- I am a marketing manager who is in transition.
- Judy Palmer, an acquaintance/colleague, passed along your name.
- John Dawson suggested that I write to you.
- We met briefly last month at
- I would like to learn more about
- I appreciate your time and expertise.
- I am interested in
- I would appreciate the opportunity to
- I have extensive experience.
- I realize your time is valuable.
- I appreciate your time and insight.
- I am sure I will benefit from your insight.
- Will value your insight

Tips

- Do not ingratiate yourself to the reader in an attempt to make an impression. It will sound unprofessional.
- Make your point quickly. If you want to meet with the reader, say that within the first two sentences.
- If a mutual acquaintance referred you to the reader, mention that person's name.
- Do not write an autobiography. Give the reader a few important, relevant details about you and your background.

Introducing Another Person

- A former colleague of mine is networking in the industry.
- I wanted to let you know that I passed your name on to
- Mike Wing, a friend of mine, is doing research on executive compensation and you would be an excellent resource for him to talk to.
- I would appreciate it if you would take a few minutes to talk with
- Her credentials are strong. For seven years, she was
- Perhaps you could explain to him how
- I know your schedule is squeezed, so I don't make this request lightly.
- I appreciate your help.
- I know your expertise will be valuable to
- Your years of experience will provide significant insight.
- He is a gracious and personable individual; I think you will like him.

Tips

- You are asking someone to do you a favor that might be time-consuming. Make the request politely.
- A complimentary remark about the person's background or distinction in the community is a nice gesture and can make the request more persuasive.

Announcing a New Location

- We are pleased to announce
- We are excited about the future at our new location.
- We will be located at
- The new site will enable us to
- Will strengthen our ability to
- Will not change
- Will not affect daily operations
- No disruption in service
- Will continue to operate
- Please be reassured that
- Will allow us to better serve you
- As a result of the move, we will be able to
- We will be expanding.
- Will continue to provide
- The same level of high-quality customer service
- Serve you in the way you are accustomed to
- Will improve our ability to
- We expect all our employees to remain with us.
- We appreciate your patience during the transition.
- We have outgrown our existing location.
- We will be easy to find.
- We apologize for any inconvenience.

Tips

- Sound enthusiastic about the move.
- Explain how the move will affect customers.
- Answer any questions that will be of particular concern to a customer.
- If some information is not available yet, say you will send a follow-up notice with the additional details.
- Mention any new products or services you will provide.

Announcing a Policy Change

- We are happy to announce
- Please note
- This change promises to
- The new policy will take effect on
- Customer satisfaction is our primary concern.
- You are welcome to
- What this policy means to customers is
- This policy will not significantly affect
- Effective immediately
- Rising costs/changes in the market have forced us to
- Previously, we
- Under the new policy
- The new policy will mean
- Not covered by the new policy is
- We understand/recognize that
- The reason for the new change is
- Several factors created the need for
- The new policy will provide customers with
- If you have questions, please call
- Customers will still be able to
- We reserve the right to change
- We are confident that this change will be a positive one.
- Several factors created the need for
- We encourage people to
- As we make the change, you will see
- Many customers have asked us to

Tips

- Clearly describe the policy and explain why it is necessary.

➤

- If this is a policy change, make clear how the new policy differs from the previous one.
- Explain to customers how they will benefit.
- Tell customers where they can get their questions answered.

Announcing a Price Increase

- To provide the same high quality, we needed to
- To remain competitive
- Because of rising costs
- We regret that we must
- We are reluctant to
- It was difficult for us to
- We appreciate your business and apologize for
- Until now, we have
- We are proud to still be
- We are among the few companies to
- On your product list, the prices that increased are
- We have seen a significant rise in the cost of our key raw materials.
- Not all the news is bad; we also have expanded our product line.
- This small increase will
- Effective June 1, our suppliers
- Please call us or write with questions.
- Many of our customers have been with us for years.
- We hope you will understand.
- We hope we can still count on your loyalty.
- Until then, we have an abundant inventory that is available at today's prices.

Tips

- Sending a letter in advance of the price increase is a courtesy that can make a customer feel special.
- Explain the reason for the increase.
- If possible, be willing to work with customers who have problems regarding the increase.

- Putting the increase in context sometimes can soften the impact of the news.

Invitation to Attend

- Please join us.
- This is your invitation to
- We invite you to
- You are invited to
- We will host a reception for
- We want to celebrate Judy's 20th anniversary at the company.
- The occasion is
- This is a fundraiser to benefit
- This will mark the 25th year that
- The event is being held on (give date, time, place)
- Dress is business casual
- Dress is semiformal
- Dress is formal
- A reception will be at 6 p.m., followed by dinner
- Following dinner, our guest speaker will be
- We hope you can attend/participate
- If you cannot attend, please contact us by
- Please bring
- Please arrive by
- Refreshments will be served
- The cost of tickets is
- Please return the enclosed card.
- To help the restaurant staff prepare, we need to know how many in your party will attend.
- If you have questions, call Pam Jones at
- To get to this location, follow Route
- We appreciate your support.
- Donations will be accepted at the door.

➡

Tips

- Not all events require formal invitations. For more casual events, handwritten invitations on note cards or stationery are fine.
- Provide specific details about the event, including the time, date, place, and appropriate dress.
- If you need to know how many people will attend, include a response card and a stamped, addressed envelope.
- When addressing the envelope and letter, you can deviate from the traditional "Mr. and Mrs. Frank Smith" format. Acceptable variations are Frank and Judy Smith, Judy and Frank Smith, Judy Johnson and Frank Smith.

Invitation to Speak

- We invite you to join us and to share with us your insight.
- You are well known in the profession/industry.
- We would appreciate the opportunity to hear your insight.
- Your name surfaced quickly.
- Dozens/hundreds of people will gather for our annual
- We would be honored
- Our members are eager to hear
- You can choose the topic.
- We are concerned about such topics/issues as
- Our group's mission is to
- We would like to hear your thoughts on
- If you can confirm
- If you are willing to join us
- I will send the details.
- After lunch, speakers usually present for an hour.
- The topic is of your choosing.
- Please let me know what you will need.

Tips

- Be sure the reader knows quickly that this is an invitation. Some writers open with promotional details to make the event sound appealing, and the invitation becomes buried.
- Tell the reader what the event is and, if necessary, why it is being held.
- Give the date, time, place, and the expected length of the presentation.
- Be complimentary of the speaker, given his or her credentials, but do not be exceedingly laudatory. Ingratiating yourself to the person in an attempt to influence the decision sounds amateurish.

Declining an Invitation

- Thank you for the invitation.
- I appreciate your thinking of me.
- Because several of your people are former colleagues of mine, I am particularly disappointed not to be able to
- Your invitation is one I would like to accept, but
- Although I would like to
- I am sorry that I cannot attend.
- Because of a conflict in my schedule
- I have another commitment.
- Because I will be out of state
- I regret that I cannot
- I am sure it will be a wonderful evening.
- I will be disappointed to miss it.
- It is unlikely that I will be available.
- Let us try again next time.
- Please let me know if I can help in the future.
- This is a difficult time.
- Ms. Jones receives hundreds of requests to speak.
- If you would like one of my colleagues to fill in

Tips

- Give your reason for not accepting the invitation, and then say no. That will help blunt the bad news and will ensure that the reader will see your explanation.
- Giving a short, courteous explanation for why you cannot accept the invitation helps to preserve goodwill, but you are not obligated to give a detailed response.
- Express your appreciation and close with a complimentary or polite comment to make it clear you are declining the invitation but are not rejecting the individual.

- Mention any specific options that you can offer.
- If you want to refer a colleague to speak instead, check first with this person to make sure it is okay to pass along his or her name.

Request for Pricing Information

- We would like to have an estimate.
- Please quote us a price for
- Please send a price list for products that
- We are in the market for ... and would appreciate a catalog and price list.
- Our current supplier is no longer carrying ... so we are seeking
- Here are the particular requirements.
- Is there a service agreement and what is the cost?
- Please provide warranty details.
- Enclosed is a stamped, addressed envelope.
- I saw the ads for [name the product], but I am unsure if that price includes
- We are interested in ... and would appreciate pricing information.
- We need ... and I hope you can help.

Tips

- Provide whatever details are necessary to make it clear to the reader what you want.
- Give the reader some sense of why you need the information.
- Edit the letter closely; be sure everything you need is included.

Responding to a Request for Something

- Last week, you wrote asking for
- Thank you for your inquiry.
- Thank you for your interest.
- Enclosed is
- Here is the information you asked for.
- I will be happy to send you
- Your new catalog is enclosed.
- We apologize that we cannot provide
- We regret that we do not have
- Although I do not know the answer, I am passing along your inquiry to
- We can schedule you for
- Perhaps there is an alternative way.
- Please let me know if I can help in some other way.
- We will let you know when it becomes available.
- Let me clarify the enclosed information.
- Although we do not have that in stock, we do have
- If you need additional
- More information is available on our Web site.
- To learn more
- Call or write if you have questions.
- Below is a list of the programs we offer.
- On Page 3 of the enclosed brochure, you will see

Tips

- State within the first two sentences exactly what you are responding to and what you are providing.
- Provide whatever explanation is needed to ensure a clear understanding.
- Response letters are an opportunity to demonstrate

➡

good customer service, thereby creating or reinforcing a good image.

- Use a courteous, professional, conversational tone.

Thank You Letter

- Thank you for your gift (name it)/help/contribution/participation/strong effort.
- I appreciate your thoughtful gift. The vase … (Mention the actual gift.)
- I appreciate the opportunity to work with you.
- Thank you for your thoughtful, detailed response to my question.
- We can't tell you how much we
- We had a delightful time.
- Thank you for taking the time to
- I want you to know how much
- My deepest thanks for
- It meant a lot to me.
- I am eager to
- Surely I will share this with
- I enjoyed working with you/your staff
- It was gracious of you to
- Your help is very much appreciated.
- Thanks for helping to make
- Your insight was helpful. Thank you for
- Never before have I been
- Fond memories
- So kind-hearted
- I am indebted.
- I will think of you each time I
- We will use the … on special occasions.
- You cannot imagine what a difference this makes.
- I will always remember
- Thank you for thinking of me/for remembering.
- On behalf of

➡

- We plan to use the [name the gift] to
- Was a special occasion
- Please stay in touch
- I look forward to

Tips

- Mention the gift or gesture that is the basis for the thank-you note, and give a few details. Say how you might use the gift, how the gesture was helpful, or how you will benefit from the meeting.
- Thank you notes in business often help to build loyalty, commitment, and enthusiasm.
- Thank you notes usually are limited to the "thank you" and a few words about the occasion. Other information or news about your life is left for a separate letter.

Congratulations Letter

- Congratulations on your award.
- You did it!
- I recently read about your promotion. Congratulations on
- I was pleased/delighted/thrilled to hear
- This is terrific news.
- This award/promotion recognizes your talent.
- This recognition reflects your tremendous attitude.
- Your contributions have inspired others.
- Your superior/outstanding performance
- You are testimony to the value of commitment and perseverance.
- You have had a major impact on
- Would not have happened without your
- This marks a milestone.
- You have persevered.
- You have distinguished yourself.
- I commend you on
- I applaud your effort and dedication.
- A long sought-after goal
- Best wishes in the future.
- Displayed the courage/discipline/foresight
- Congratulations on opening your own
- With your experience and wisdom, I am sure
- To your credit
- Earned the respect
- Your record/performance is impressive.

Tips

- If you are congratulating someone who earned recognition, say what you honestly feel but do not be

➡

42

excessive in your praise; it sounds phony.

- Be specific, not vague. Refer to the achievement by name, cite what the person did to reach the goal, and perhaps mention a related experience that the two of you shared in the past.
- Keep the focus on the reader. Do not begin discussing similar achievements of your own.
- Consider your relationship with the reader. Avoid sounding too chummy or casual if the relationship is purely professional. Avoid humor that might not be appreciated.

Chapter 3

Specific Types of Business Letters

Specific Letters

Letters are often the most effective vehicle for such specific functions as selling products and services, applying for employment, responding to customer concerns, fostering goodwill, and collecting money. A letter is longer than an e-mail, the ideas contained in a letter are more carefully and clearly presented than in a note card or in a voice message, and the letter is often more personalized.

Remember that a business letter always reflects back on you, the writer, and on the company. It is your personality and the company's that come off the page as the reader processes the information. No matter what the issue, your letter should have a courteous, professional tone that leaves the reader with a positive impression.

Whether you are asking someone to do something, apologizing to a customer, or complaining to a colleague, your letter should be focused, clear on one reading, and tightly written.

Sales Letter: Introducing Yourself

- Our mutual friend Jack Hennessey passed along your name. I am a sales representative for

- We met briefly last month at the sales convention reception. I am a representative with the WhirlyGig Company.

- I am a new member of the sales staff at Medical Diagnostics and would like to introduce myself.

- I succeeded Cindy Clements and am now responsible for this territory.

- I would appreciate the opportunity to come by and say hello and talk with you about your needs.

- I joined the company after five years at Statewide Health, and I have extensive experience in

- Although I know you already have a relationship with a supplier, I would appreciate the chance to show you our new

- Our company has undergone several changes in the past year.

- With the additional administrative demands accompanying your rapid growth, you might be interested to learn about the new (name product) that we offer.

- I look forward to meeting you.

- If there is anything I can do, please call or write anytime.

Tips

- The purpose of the letter is to let a customer know that someone new is covering the account and that you want to introduce yourself.

- Express interest in the account, and if you know some tidbit of news about the customer or the industry,

➡

mention that; it shows you do your homework.
- Tell the reader a little about yourself.
- Make it clear you stand ready to serve the customer.

Sales Letter: Cold Call

- A friend of mine whom you know, Pam Sears, passed along your name. I am a sales representative for
- I saw you from a distance at the sales convention last month but was unable to say hello, so I thought I would send you a note.
- I am an account representative for MedTech Corp., and we manufacture medical devices for
- I would appreciate the opportunity to come by and introduce myself to see if our products might fit your needs.
- I succeeded Lori Roberts and am now responsible for this territory.
- I would like to learn more about your company and your needs in case I can help.
- I have been in sales for 14 years, most recently with
- Although I know you already have a relationship with a supplier, I would appreciate the opportunity to say hello and tell you a little about the products we have that might interest you.
- Our company has undergone several changes in the past year.
- With your company growing rapidly and facing increasing demands for new technology, you might be interested to learn about two new products that we offer.
- I look forward to meeting you.
- In the interim, if I can be of help, please call me.

Tips

- Introduce yourself and say you would like to meet, or perhaps a phone conversation might suffice.

- Show that you know something already about the company.
- Tell the reader a little about yourself.
- Make it clear you stand ready to serve the customer.
- Try to find out more about their specific needs and show how you can fill them.

Sales Letter: Follow-Up to Previous Letter

- We met last month at the conference in Chicago.
- I am the marketing manager who wrote to you back in the spring about
- A few years ago, I wrote to you asking for your suggestions.
- Earlier this year, we wrote to you about … We thought we would follow up to ask.
- I am following up on my message of [give a month or specific date] to make sure you have what you need.
- I thought I would reconnect with you, following our discussion two weeks ago, to offer another possibility.
- Thank you for meeting with me.
- I appreciate your passing along the information about
- The information you sent was great.
- Thank you for your offering to send … I look forward to seeing it.
- Your wisdom and insight were immensely helpful.
- I realize that your schedule is crammed, but I still would be interested to receive … when you get a chance.
- I know that messages sometimes get lost, so I thought I would follow up to ask if you
- I assume that you have been buried in other issues since we spoke three weeks ago, so I thought I would follow up.
- Here is what has changed/what is new.
- Thank you again, and I will stay in touch.
- I will finish this as soon as I receive your thoughts and suggestions.
- I appreciate your help and hope we can talk further.
- If I have further questions, I hope I can call on you again for insight.
- Just a reminder. Please send me

➡

Tips

- Do not open with abundant background information. Make it clear it is a follow-up letter or memo, briefly mention the earlier note, and quickly state the purpose of this message.
- After stating the purpose of the new message, briefly restate the essence of the earlier note to refresh the person's memory.
- Look for ways to eliminate needless words. Avoid opening a follow-up note with "I would like to take this opportunity to thank you … "The first eight words contribute nothing; state the sentence at "Thank you … "
- Avoid being blunt, even if you have waited a long time for a response. Give the reader the benefit of the doubt. Even thoughtful, generous people inadvertently forget or overlook tasks.

Sales Letter: To New Customers

- I want to welcome you as one of our new customers.
- We are pleased to have you on board.
- We specialize in
- As a customer, you will receive periodic product updates.
- Please call or send me an e-mail anytime.
- We are here to serve you.
- Enclosed is information about our services.
- Your sales representative, Janet Palmer, will be in touch.
- We have a strong record of providing quality service.
- We appreciate your
- I look forward to learning more about your company.
- I wish you well in getting your new business established.
- I look forward to a long relationship.

Tips

- Whenever possible, personalize the letter by mentioning something particular about the customer's business.
- Let customers know what they can expect to receive from you in the form of service.
- Tell the reader you are pleased and gratified that she has chosen your company and that your staff is ready to help.

Sales Letter:
New Product Announcement

- We are introducing
- Enclosed is detailed literature on
- A new whirlygig that will enable you to work more efficiently is being introduced today.
- Finally, a product that is specially designed for the type of technology that you use.
- Meets the new federal standards, which require that
- Has the following features:
- Several other prominent companies are using it.
- An updated version
- Because of the volume of business you do with us, we are offering
- If this has been a problem for you, I/we can help.
- You will be impressed by
- High-quality material

Tips

- The opening sentence should say what the product is, capture the essence of what it does, and say who will benefit.
- Add additional detail about how the product could be useful to a customer.
- Say when and where the new product will be available.
- Emphasize the benefits, and clearly distinguish between the benefits and the features. Also make it clear what the full impact for the customer will be.

Sales Letter: To Win Back or Regain Inactive Customer

- It has been a year since you last ordered
- It has been more than a year since we last spoke.
- If something displeased you, please let us know.
- I am always concerned when we lose a good customer.
- Please let me know if there was something you were unhappy with
- We did not do a training program the past two years, so I am wondering if you might be interested in
- I thought I would reconnect with you to let you know about our new services.
- I want to be sure that we meet your expectations.
- Please call me, send me an e-mail, or use the enclosed envelope to write me a short note explaining what happened.
- If your absence has been because of a backlog of work, please call me or write when you get a chance.
- Our business has grown and changed since we last spoke. We now offer
- I apologize for the error that caused your dissatisfaction.
- Our staff and our administrative practices have changed since your unfortunate experience.
- We would appreciate the chance to renew our relationship.
- I see that your business has expanded considerably. Congratulations.

Tips

- Give an update on any significant new customers you might have and any new products or services you offer. ➥

- Express your concern and disappointment that the customer has not done business with your company for a while.
- Make it clear you would like to hear what the problem is, in the interests of mending the relationship.

Sales Letter: Trade Show Follow-Up

- We met last month at the New York trade show.
- I thoroughly enjoyed talking with you at the trade show last week.
- I thought I would reconnect with you, following our discussion two weeks ago.
- I can offer an additional option to the two we talked about.
- Thank you for coming by the booth.
- Enclosed is the information I said I would send about
- Attached are the workshop outlines you asked about at the trade show last week.
- You asked for specific details about the TickleToys, so I am enclosing a product sheet.
- I appreciate your stopping by our booth at the trade show.
- We are the industry's No. 1 maker of
- Please keep us in mind.

Tips

- Quickly make reference to where you met the reader so that the reader has context for the message.
- Capture the essence of your company and its products.
- Refer to any particular topic you and the reader might have talked about at the trade show.
- Ask the reader to keep in touch, and say you will follow up in six months or any other specific amount of time.
- Keep the letter or e-mail message brief. You goal is to reconnect with the reader and stay on his or her radar screen; do not be long-winded.

Customer Service Letter:
Apology to Customer

- Thank you for bringing … to our attention.
- I was disturbed to learn
- As I understand it, you received
- We apologize for
- I am sorry for the misunderstanding.
- I regret the mistake.
- It should not have happened.
- Please accept my apology.
- Please forgive me for
- I mistakenly presumed that
- We are checking to see.
- I have spoken with her.
- It was shortsighted of me.
- Let me explain what happened.
- We are taking immediate steps to prevent this.
- To ensure that it does not happen again, we
- I should have checked more closely.
- This was an oversight, but it was inexcusable.
- I pride myself in careful attention to detail.
- We take great pride in our customer service.
- We appreciate your business.
- You have been a loyal customer, and we value your friendship.
- I/We accept responsibility for
- I appreciate your understanding.
- Please call me to discuss this.
- We will credit you with
- I will replace

➡

Tips

- Heartfelt apologies can be significantly helpful in mending social and business relationships.
- Stay focused on this particular occurrence. Apologize, pledge to correct the problem, and thank the customer for his or her business.
- You can explain what happened, though in many cases, it is not necessary to go into detail.
- Do not make excuses, and definitely do not try to shift the blame to the reader so that you can shed responsibility for it.

Customer Service Letter: Apology for a Delayed Order

- We apologize for the delay.
- Because the warehouse does not have the product in stock, your order has been delayed.
- Unexpected delays
- This is our problem.
- We acknowledge that we
- I am sorry that I cannot cancel delivery.
- We cannot deliver as promptly as we hoped, but we can deliver them by
- Your order is on the way.
- We are awaiting delivery of
- Because of weather-related delays in the East/Midwest/West/South
- I want you to know of the delay in advance so that you can
- We will monitor the order and will tell you when it is scheduled to arrive.
- We apologize for the unavoidable delay.
- We know this is a setback.
- We can provide part of the order now.
- We apologize for any inconvenience.
- It is troubling.
- Here is an alternative.
- In the meantime, let us know if we can help in any way.
- Although delays are common in business, we try diligently to avoid them.
- We pride ourselves in prompt delivery.
- Complete satisfaction
- You have been a loyal customer, and we value the relationship.

➡

- We appreciate your understanding.
- We hope we can look forward to your continued business.

Tips

- Apologize sincerely for the delay and move on; do not saturate the message with apologetic wording.
- Do not use excuses that customers have seen or heard many times before, such as an equipment malfunction.
- Express your regret, explain the issue, ask if there is anything you can do, and say you are grateful for the customer's business.

Customer Service Letter: To Regain Customer's Confidence

- Thank you for your letter.
- I appreciate your letting us know about
- We take great pride in our customer service.
- We appreciate your business.
- You have been a long-time customer, and we appreciate your support.
- The fact that this happened disturbs me.
- We will do whatever we can to ensure that you are satisfied.
- You can return the (product) to us.
- I looked into what happened, and I learned that
- I have asked our product manager, Pam Jones, to call you to explain what happened and to find out what we can do.
- It is important to me that you be pleased.
- We have made a few changes to ensure that this does not happen again.
- I understand how disappointing/disturbing/frustrating this must have been.
- We are extending to you a discount.
- I regret the mistake.
- It should not have happened.
- Please accept my apology.
- I have spoken with her.
- To ensure that it does not happen again, we
- This was an oversight, and it should not have happened.
- I/We accept responsibility for
- I appreciate your understanding.
- You are welcome to call me to discuss this further.
- We will ship you ➡

- Again, my sincere apology. I hope that we can look forward to working with you in the years ahead.

Tips

- Say that you appreciate the person notifying you and that you truly are concerned about the problem.
- State clearly what you will do to help the customer.
- Explain what happened but do not dole out excuses; the reader is not interested. It is your problem. Accept responsibility for it, and pledge to do whatever you can to prevent it from recurring.

Complaint Letter: To a Vendor/Supplier

- I am concerned about
- I was disturbed to see
- Last month, we ordered
- Our employees have found it difficult.
- The project proposal laid out
- This does not appear to be consistent with
- What can we do to correct the problem?
- I don't want to have to cancel.
- We have enjoyed a long-standing relationship, but
- This type of misunderstanding makes it difficult for us.
- I was under the impression that we had agreed on
- Those who attended your training class were expecting
- The reason this is difficult is
- In our previous discussions, we said
- My expectation was that
- We have customers/employees who expect
- When will you know?
- I appreciate your attention to this.
- What alternatives can you suggest?
- I want to work with you.
- The effort is not up to standard.
- I appreciate your effort. However,

Tips

- Be tactful. Make your point, firmly if necessary, depending on the seriousness of the problem, but do not be harshly critical or sarcastic. Exercise restraint.
- If possible, precede the complaint with something positive about the vendor, his or her business, or your relationship.

➡

- Focus on the particular subject you are complaining about today; avoid mentioning previous complaints or other peripheral issues.
- Keep the complaint between you and the vendor (your immediate contact) initially. Do not "cc" anyone, because it will appear that you are trying to intimidate the reader.

Complaint Letter: To an Employee

- I would appreciate it if
- You are capable of
- Our department/team is successful when we all
- You can help.
- Please explain.
- I hope you will consider
- Please tell me how I can help.
- I am here to help.
- Our policy is … However, I have noticed recently
- What I would like to see is
- Is not consistent with our customary practice of
- We are trying to build an atmosphere of
- I hope this can be a learning experience.
- Your colleagues will find it helpful.
- We need to work as a team.
- I am interested in learning.
- I hope we can move ahead.
- Can you suggest the next step?
- What do you have for ideas?

Tips

- Be empathetic. Make your point, firmly if necessary, depending on the seriousness of the problem, but exercise restraint.
- Be positive, emphasize that you are "in this together" and that you are there to help.
- Focus on the behavior, not on the person. Do not denigrate the individual.
- Open with a neutral statement that the reader cannot argue with, and perhaps even be positive, with a

compliment about the person's overall performance. Express your complaint, and then exit on an upbeat note, offering to help and move on.

Response to Complaint Letter: When You Are Not at Fault

- Thank you for your letter expressing your disappointment.
- I understand your frustration.
- We regret that you had trouble.
- We take pride in ensuring
- We guarantee our product/work.
- Which is contained in the directions
- I looked into what happened, and I learned that
- I apologize for the misunderstanding/ miscommunication.
- We were under the impression that
- We appreciate your business and are ready to work with you again.
- What I can offer you is
- The work order, which we and you signed, states that
- Our company policy in these instances is to
- The information that you provided indicated
- Our quality-control department checked the [product name] but found no flaw.
- I appreciate your letting us know about
- We take great pride in our customer service.
- We appreciate your business.
- You have been a long-time customer, and we appreciate your support.

Tips

- Thank the person for writing about the problem.
- Be courteous. Do not sound pompous and condescending because you are not at fault.
- Maintain a neutral tone, and stick to the facts. ➡

- Do not imply that the reader shares the blame, even if he or she does.
- Explain why you are not at fault, but be careful not to start giving excuses.

Response to Complaint Letter: When the Company Is at Fault

- We inadvertently sent you
- We will not charge you for
- We are sorry to hear about
- I understand your disappointment/ frustration.
- Enclosed is
- Thank you for correcting us on the accuracy of
- We apologize for this unusual occurrence.
- We will swap this for a new one and will send it.
- We are committed to high-quality customer service.
- That should not have happened.
- We have high standards for
- We are willing to
- Want to be responsive
- You are correct.
- Not to your liking
- Rarely happens
- We are taking steps to ensure that
- Will replace it
- Enclosed is a coupon for
- We regret the error
- Wish to rectify the situation
- Please call us if you have questions.
- You are a loyal customer.
- We appreciate your business and hope that
- I apologize for the inconvenience.
- Thank you for your patience.

Tips

- Express your regret but do not be excessive.

Apologizing several times is overkill.

- Accept responsibility for the error; do not imply that the customer shares the blame.

- Say you hope to continue to enjoy the customer's business.

- Be careful about such phrasing as "sorry for the flaw you discovered," because it implies that there was a flaw. Consult with your company's legal counsel on any potential product liability issues.

Letter of Apology:
For an Attitude or an Error

- My reaction/attitude was inappropriate.
- I apologize for
- Next time, I will
- I should have realized.
- Such a mistake reflects inattention to detail.
- To prevent a similar mistake next time
- It should not have happened.
- Please accept my apology.
- Please forgive me for
- My comments lacked forethought.
- I realize that I need to be more sensitive to
- What I should have done was
- I mistakenly presumed that
- It was shortsighted of me.
- I failed to consider
- I should have thought it through.
- I reacted too quickly.
- I know that my actions were troubling.
- I hope that we can discuss this and put it behind us.
- Please let me know what I can do.
- Please tell me what I can do make this up to you.
- I am open to suggestions for resolving this.
- In the interests of the team
- I realize the importance of
- I neglected to … and I am sorry.
- Please understand.
- To make up for my error in judgment, I can

➡

Tips

- Heartfelt apologies are a powerful way to convey your regret, and it is a significant step toward reconciling with the person offended.
- Apologize upfront in the message, and do not couch your apology in language intended to put part of the blame on others.
- Explain briefly what happened, and say what you will do to prevent it from happening again.
- Apologies are no longer credible when the behavior occurs repeatedly.

Letter of Apology: For Being Late

- I should not have scheduled meetings so closely.
- I realize the importance of such a meeting/event/occasion.
- I neglected to
- To make up for the time I missed, I am willing to
- I apologize for
- It should not have happened.
- Please accept my apology.
- Please forgive me for being late.
- I mistakenly presumed that
- It was poor planning on my part.
- Let me explain what happened.
- Next time, I will

Tips

- People appreciate sincere apologies. They go a long way toward soothing hurt feelings or irritation.
- Apologize, pledge to correct the problem, and thank the reader for his or her understanding.
- A brief explanation of why a person was late is appropriate, though usually not mandatory.
- Avoid making excuses. Do not blame tardiness on a busy schedule or on an alarm clock not going off. Accept responsibility and move on.
- Apologies lose their value when people are repeatedly late. Habitual tardiness damages credibility and could lead to more serious consequences.

Letter Requesting a Leave of Absence

- I would like to be considered.
- I am applying for
- For personal reasons
- I would like to return on
- Would appreciate the opportunity to return
- If the company would hold my position open
- Paid/unpaid leave
- My absence will begin on
- I intend to return on
- During this time, my benefits will/will not
- Pension fund contributions will be interrupted.
- To take advantage of
- To pursue an educational opportunity
- For years, I have desired to
- In recent months
- I appreciate your cooperation/support.
- Approve/grant my request

Tips

- The letter can be short because in most cases the topic already has been discussed with your supervisor. The letter makes it official.
- State briefly why you are requesting the leave.
- Make it clear that you understand the implications of taking a leave.
- Convey your interest in maintaining your relationship with the company.
- Express your appreciation.

Letter of Sympathy

- I am sorry to hear about
- I was so sorry to hear of
- I share in your sorrow.
- We were saddened at the loss of
- We lost a great friend.
- She had a great impact on
- He was a special person.
- She was always smiling.
- No one ever did so much to
- She was a joy to know.
- My thoughts are with you.
- I wish there were words to express
- He has a special place in our hearts and minds.
- She will be sadly missed.
- May you find strength in knowing that
- Our sympathies at this time of deep loss
- We have the memories to sustain us.
- A feeling of emptiness
- I remember how much I enjoyed talking with her about
- She brought such warmth and humor to her friends.
- Like most people, I was stunned.
- In this most difficult time
- Although I did not know her, I heard about her often.

Tips

- Most letters of condolence are short. The fact that you write is what is important; many people, feeling helpless, do nothing.
- Avoid messages that are overly religious, sentimental, or personal.

➡

- Mention a particular quality or anecdote that you remember from the person's past.

Letter of Termination

- We regret that this action is necessary.
- At that time, I notified you
- Problems with your performance
- On Oct. 4, we discussed … Following that,
- Repeated absences
- Has happened repeatedly
- This is not the first time.
- Failure to meet expectations
- Failure to comply
- You did not respond.
- Employment has been terminated.
- Effective immediately
- Your history with the company has been
- We have tried
- Have been given numerous opportunities
- You are aware
- Such conduct is unacceptable.
- Is inappropriate
- According to company policy
- This company does not tolerate
- You should be familiar with
- We verified that
- These actions constitute
- Job performance has been unsatisfactory/unacceptable.
- Unauthorized use of
- These are grounds for dismissal.
- Violated company policy
- An obvious violation of
- Must notify a supervisor
- You leave the company no choice but to

➡

- You will receive the pension you have accrued.
- Please contact the human resources department to make arrangements to receive the compensation and benefits that are due to you.

Tips

- There is no "one size fits all" for termination letters. Every employee's situation is different, and it is personal.
- Clearly explain what has led to the termination.
- Stay focused on the facts. Avoid letting innuendo and opinion seep in.
- Do not be disrespectful or sarcastic.

Letter Requesting Donations or Sponsorship

- Our organization is hosting [name the event] and would appreciate your support.
- Our organization has provided thousands of people with opportunities to
- It would be wonderful if we could reach more people.
- Your tax-deductible donation will help us buy
- With your support, more children will have
- Will help to defray the cost of
- We would be grateful if you would contribute the refreshments.
- In exchange for donating the soda, your company logo will be displayed.
- Will increase your visibility before an audience of
- This annual event raises money for
- The money we raise will be dedicated to
- Last year, we raised
- In exchange for your donation, we will
- This event will put your name in front of hundreds of retailers.
- Will provide your company with significant exposure
- We would appreciate it if you would contribute two gift certificates to our raffle.
- You will be recognized.
- For two decades, you have been a leader in our community.
- We appreciate your generosity.
- Our organization has been sustained by the thoughtful support of companies like yours.
- I encourage you to be part of
- We have four options for sponsorship.
- You can donate in several ways.

➡

Tips

- Make it clear what your organization is, whom it represents, and what the event is about.
- Be clear about the benefit to the person donating or sponsoring.
- Do not merely ask for a donation if you have something specific in mind: money, products, office space, equipment.
- The appeal can include a cover letter and a page or two of more specific information, if appropriate, about the event and about sponsorship opportunities.
- Name other prominent people who are participating or who have in the past.

Letter Turning Down a Donation Request

- Thank you for your letter, but because we receive many requests
- Our company receives hundreds of requests for donations.
- We give one block donation to the city's Charitable Trust, which reaches many groups.
- We target our contributions to the county's schools.
- Is not compatible with our criteria
- Does not fit with our requirements
- Is not consistent with our company's philosophy
- Yours is a worthy cause.
- I wish we could respond favorably to your request.
- Although I wish we could honor your request
- Your organization does great work.
- Please accept our regrets.
- We wish you the best with your endeavor.
- I regret that we cannot.
- Please try us again another time.

Tips

- Decline politely and give a credible reason for saying no, but you do not need to elaborate.
- Be professionally conversational; try to avoid a stiff, cold corporate tone.

Reference Letters:
Asking for a Letter of Recommendation

- I would like to take you up on your offer to write me a letter of reference.
- I am applying for a position as a marketing manager and would appreciate a letter of reference.
- You are a person of distinction in the industry, and you are familiar with my work.
- We have worked well together.
- I have enjoyed having you as a client and hope that I can use your name as a reference.
- I would appreciate the opportunity to offer your name as a reference.
- You recently offered to write me a letter of reference.
- Thank you for your willingness to write me a letter of recommendation.
- Please address what my managing philosophy is and how I work with people.
- Perhaps you will find it helpful if I explain what the position entails.
- High on the list of requirements for this position is/are
- I appreciate your help.
- Thank you for your support.
- Thank you very much for the letter.

Tips

- Make it clear that you do not want to put the person in an uncomfortable position, but that you would appreciate a letter of recommendation.
- Tell the writer about the job you are seeking and about the company.

➥

- If the job description lists requirements that are particularly well suited to your skill set, mention those to the person writing the reference letter.

Reference Letters: Giving a Recommendation

- I have known the candidate for years.
- I wholeheartedly endorse
- I am happy to support her candidacy.
- It is my pleasure to recommend
- He frequently participated in
- A positive experience
- She was among my top employees.
- He was a delight to work with.
- You could not ask for a person more dedicated.
- Has always been reliable
- Is a professional in every sense of the word
- Her demonstrated leadership
- Has leadership abilities/qualities
- Was enthusiastic and diligent
- Had a positive presence
- A joy to work with
- Self-motivator/self-starter
- Good communicator
- She was a central figure in
- Was instrumental
- He played a critical role in
- Displayed initiative
- A good listener
- Unselfish
- Sensitive toward colleagues
- Is focused and goal oriented
- Strong sense of purpose
- Highly respected by colleagues
- Although Ray is enthusiastic and diligent, he occasionally needs to take greater care in

➡

- Linda's genuine interest in helping people achieve excellence sometimes leads to impatience.
- Could be more consistent
- Needs to recognize/to be more mindful of
- She can help herself if she realizes
- The more tactful he is, the more likely he is to get the results he wants.
- Is better suited for
- Will perform best in an environment where

Tips

- Give specific details to improve the person's chances of getting the job.
- Write efficiently—tight and to the point—to ensure that the letter is read.
- Base the letter on factual information that you know from your own experience working with the person.

Reminder Letter

- I realize that your schedule is crammed, but I want to remind you of
- I know that you have a lot happening right now, but when you get a chance, please
- You mentioned in your note last month that you would send
- I want to let you know that
- The board meeting is next week, so I thought I would send you
- I still am interested in seeing the samples that you said last week you had.
- This is a reminder that the meeting time has changed.
- The deadline for recommending candidates is only three days away.
- The move to our new headquarters will begin on Monday.
- I appreciate your offer last month to send me
- I look forward to getting it, as soon as you have a chance.
- I thought you would appreciate a reminder.
- I want to make sure you remember.
- To ensure that your staff is included in… we need to receive
- You probably have the Friday night reception on your calendar, but I thought I would
- I thought I would check to see if
- We still have your [name the item]. The secretary has it, whenever you want to pick it up.

Tips

- Politely nudge the reader, but do not sound impatient. This is, after all, a friendly reminder; it is not a reprimand for violating a policy.

- If the person said she would do something, mention specifically, if possible, what she said, when she said it, and whether it was in a memo, e-mail, voice mail, or conversation.

Chapter 4

Memos

Memos are the standard document for communicating internally in organizations, and they take the form of Word documents and e-mail messages. People sometimes are under the illusion that they do not write memos, only e-mail. But any message about substantive daily business issues and activities is a memo and should be distinguished from a two-sentence e-mail message about going to lunch.

Information in a memo can be organized in any of several formats. A descending order of importance (main points first) is the most common, an indirect approach (for bad news) eases into the main point, a sequential order is appropriate when walking the reader through steps, and a chronological order is common for historical information.

An important but seldom-taught technique for memos is to open with a summary paragraph, generally two to four sentences that capture the essence of the message. You often will return to these topics in more detail further down in the message, but by mentioning the key points in the first paragraph, the reader gets an immediate snapshot of what the message is all about, which helps to focus the person's attention.

If the memo is sent as a Word document, label the opening paragraph "Summary" or "Overview," in a bold, underlined heading. In an e-mail message, you might not use headings, but the opening paragraph still should capture the highlights that the reader must know to understand the point of the message.

Announcing a New Policy

- We are announcing a new policy.
- Effective June 1, you will
- The new policy will take effect on
- The purpose of the policy is to ensure that
- Although the existing policy was appropriate and effective during that time, it is now
- Please note that you will need the new ID card for entry into
- Please read the policy carefully.
- Please review the information.
- This memo summarizes the new benefits policy.
- The most important elements of this policy are
- We have tried [previous method] in the past but have been unsuccessful, so we thought this time
- We invite your feedback.
- You are welcome to suggest
- What this policy means to customers is
- This policy will not significantly affect
- Rising costs/changes in the market have forced us to
- Previously, we
- Under this policy
- The new policy will mean
- Not covered by the new policy is
- We understand/recognize that
- The policy will help to
- Several factors created the need for
- The new policy will enable employees/customers to
- You will still be able to
- We reserve the right to change
- We are confident that this change will be a positive one. ➡

- Several factors created the need for
- We encourage people to
- As we implement the policy, you will see
- Many people have asked us to

Tips

- Clearly describe the policy, and explain why it is necessary and what the expectations are.
- If people will see a direct benefit, say that.
- If the policy will significantly affect people in their daily business activities, say what the impact will be.
- Tell people where they can get their questions answered.

Providing Routine Information

- In response to your request, I am sending
- Here is the information you asked for.
- Please be aware.
- Enclosed/attached is
- In the attached memo, I explain
- Below are suggestions for
- Is receptive to these ideas
- It will be helpful.
- It would be beneficial to
- Is responsible for
- Please send me
- Please report back to me.
- Please review.
- This is only a draft; the phrasing and some content will change as we develop it.
- This is just a preliminary list.
- These are my initial thoughts.
- Please send any comments or concerns you might have.
- I want to help you develop a plan to accomplish the goal.
- Attached is an analysis of
- We decided/determined that
- Before I send the information, I need to know
- Your request did not indicate
- I want to pass along

Tips

- Tell the reader quickly why you are writing and what is contained in your message.
- If you have three or four topics to cover, tell the reader that in the opening paragraph. Address the topics in ➡

the body of the message in the same order that you mentioned them in the first paragraph. The reader can easily follow the logic of the message.

- Provide the essential information and perhaps a little additional explanation, but avoid too much surplus information. It obscures your message, and it is a disservice to a busy reader.
- Be sure all the reader's questions are answered.

Conveying Sensitive News about a Merger or Layoffs

- Most of you are aware that
- Because we no longer have that contract, we are forced to
- After assessing/evaluating
- We concluded that
- To remain competitive, we must
- The reason these changes are necessary is
- I appreciate your contributions; however
- We face significant challenges.
- In reaching this decision, I considered
- We considered several options.
- Ease the transition
- Would jeopardize our
- To meet this goal, we
- The changes will mean
- We have no choice but to
- Our only realistic option is to
- We appreciate your effort and your attitude.
- I realize that this means significant changes for
- We will meet with
- Several factors made this step necessary.
- We already have tried to
- We have seen/experienced
- It is clear that
- For these reasons, there was no alternative.
- Please let me know if I can
- Your commitment was significant, and I appreciate
- You invested a lot of yourself.
- Will be eligible for
- We are making every effort to

➡

- Please come talk to me if you have questions.
- We will be happy to help you find
- We do not expect
- Should the situation change

Tips

- Be sensitive to the impact of the announcement on the readers.
- Be candid when announcing a merger, reorganization, or layoffs. Tell the reader(s) as much as possible about what is happening and what the impact will be. Candor will have an enduring benefit; you will be viewed as credible and trustworthy by the employees who remain.
- Explain how management reached its decision, and state the business case for the action.
- Express your disappointment and regret, and say what services and benefits will be available to help employees.
- Tell the audience what is scheduled to happen next and give realistic time frames.

Conveying Disappointing News

- I know this is disappointing.
- Perhaps as an alternative
- You have made a terrific contribution.
- You are an asset to our department.
- In reaching this decision, I considered
- I cannot recommend
- It is difficult to accept that.
- I find it difficult to support the notion that
- We appreciate your effort and your attitude.
- I looked for someone with the exact experience and skills that are needed.
- Having said that, we still can
- Here is what I can suggest.
- This does not mean
- Perhaps another opportunity will arise.
- Your abilities and leadership are best suited for
- Please let me know if I can suggest options.
- I will keep your proposal.
- Your commitment was significant, and I appreciate
- You invested a lot of yourself.
- The more I studied the criteria/requirements, the more I became convinced.
- In examining the complexities of the project, I realized
- Can you suggest the next step?
- This has been a valuable experience.
- Please let me know if you have other ideas.
- Here is how you can improve your proposal/chances for approval.
- One factor that you might consider
- I am sorry that I cannot be more encouraging.

➡

Tips

- Make it clear what your answer is; do not sound hazy.
- Open with a statement that is positive and perhaps complimentary, but at least neutral, something that the reader cannot take issue with. Convey the disappointing news and then exit with a positive or neutral statement.
- Have a polite, respectful tone. Be sensitive, never rude, sarcastic, or demeaning. Remember that the person is still a colleague or a customer.
- Express your disappointment in not being able to provide positive news, and try to be helpful.

Asking Reader to Do Something

- Please consider
- I would appreciate it if you could
- I appreciate your help.
- The reason I need your help is
- Because of a change in plans, we are scrambling and would appreciate your help.
- This is significant because
- I realize you have a crammed schedule.
- This will provide a great opportunity.
- Your help is needed.
- Your help can make this a success.
- By doing this, you will
- Here is why this will make a difference.
- There are several compelling reasons.
- The staff needs your help/guidance/leadership/expertise.
- The staff faces significant challenges.
- Would like to attend
- A rare professional development opportunity
- The committee has endorsed this.
- I hope you can help.
- Can you meet with Ray to discuss
- I am asking for this because
- Do not hesitate to ask for help.
- Here is what I am asking you to do.
- After you have finished that step
- The deadline is
- The most important thing to remember is
- You can find more information on our intranet site at

➡

Tips

- Be clear about what you need, why you need it, and what the person has to do to comply.
- If it is appropriate, say specifically why you are asking this particular person for the favor.
- Be sure to include all the important details, including dates, places, and times.
- Present the deadline early in the message; do not assume the reader will read to the end.

Announcing a Change in an Existing Policy

- After hearing from many employees, we've determined
- We reviewed our existing way of doing things.
- We/the committee assessed the value of
- Identified changes that are needed
- Has built-in flexibility
- I am happy to announce
- We regret that we no longer can allow
- Our goal is to
- We are pleased that this will mean
- Effective immediately
- The major changes are
- Although this is not a radical departure from current policy, it will mean
- This revised policy applies to
- Given recent events, we need to
- Because of the recent circumstances
- Several factors prompted us to make this change.
- Under the previous policy
- Our policy in the past has been to
- Our practice has been to allow … but recent events have forced us to
- Because of changes in
- To ensure that all employees have … we are revising our policy.
- I am asking that each person
- This policy change is an important element of our plan/program/effort.
- We are committed to
- We are confident that you will see the long-term benefit.
- If all of us contribute

- This will be a significant step toward
- This will enable us to
- Those who will be affected are
- Although some initial adjustment will
- We realize that this will require some changes.
- We know that the revised policy will pose a challenge.
- We've decided to make the difficult decision to
- New skills will be needed.
- Will implement the policy over a few months
- We apologize for any inconvenience.
- We appreciate your support and cooperation.
- This change is consistent with our attempts to
- We need to maintain high standards.
- Need to take these precautions because
- If you have questions, please call.

Tips

- Make clear what the policy change is and how the new policy differs from the old one.
- Explain why the change was necessary.
- Say how employees will benefit.
- Give the effective date of the change.
- Provide a resource and phone number or e-mail address for people with questions.

Announcing a New Program

- We are pleased to introduce
- With our continuing push for
- As part of our effort to offer
- The program will begin
- Effective Sept. 1, you will be able to
- We created the program to give employees
- This new program will provide a great opportunity for people to
- Our objective is to
- In this memo are/attached are the details of the program.
- Many employees were asking for
- The new program will provide several benefits.
- Under this program, you will be permitted to
- Is open to all employees
- Those who are eligible are
- To participate in the program, you need to
- You will be expected to
- People who enroll will
- As a participant, your commitment is to
- There is no requirement.
- You are not obligated to
- Need to maintain a high level of performance
- To achieve our goals
- The purpose/aim of the program is to
- Please review the material.
- Additional details are available on our Web site.
- The program underscores our commitment to
- Demonstrates/signifies the importance we attach to

➡

Tips

- Clearly describe the program and what it means to employees or customers.
- Say why the program is being offered.
- State where, when, and how to sign up.
- Tell people where they can get their questions answered.

Announcing a Meeting

- We will meet next Tuesday.
- In preparation for
- To help us understand …, we will meet
- At the meeting, [your goals] will be explained/outlined/ discussed.
- To make the meeting more productive, I am attaching an agenda.
- Please plan to meet Friday at
- We want to hear your suggestions.
- The main topics to be covered are
- Here are the key issues we face:
- The purpose/objectives of the meeting is/are to
- We need to develop recommendations for
- Please consider
- Please think about the following list of questions and come ready to discuss
- Present some creative ideas
- Please come prepared to say
- Attached is an agenda.
- Providing you with this information in advance will help you to focus your thinking.
- If you cannot attend, please contact me by phone or e-mail.
- The meeting is particularly important for those who are
- After this meeting, our next step will be to
- We will meet again to discuss remaining issues.

Tips

- Explain the purpose of the meeting and the reason it is significant. When most people receive meeting notices, they immediately try to think of reasons not to go.

➡

- Say what you hope to accomplish in the meeting.
- State when and where the meeting will be held.
- Provide your contact information in case people cannot attend or have questions.

Status Report

- I am pleased to report that
- To let you know the status of
- To bring you up to date on the status of our project, we completed
- I recently met with ... and explained
- Should be finished by
- Within the budget
- After extensive research, we found
- The key highlight is that we learned X but still need to determine Y.
- We are progressing.
- To be effective, we need to
- We recommend
- At the close of this quarter
- I am optimistic about
- Solid performance
- For months, we have seen
- Recent results confirmed that
- We are now
- Had some concerns
- Indications are that
- To meet our goal, we have
- They need
- We met with
- This needs to be a priority.
- Should consider other possibilities
- Perhaps we can discuss
- Need to study alternatives
- We are pleased with the progress of

➡

Tips

- Capture in the first paragraph the most important highlights about the status or progress of the project or activity. Do not go into detail; you can return to these topics later in the memo and elaborate there.

- Do not begin the opening sentence with "The purpose of this memo is to bring you up to date on the status of ... " because it tells the reader nothing. Say in the subject line "status report on our budget discussions" or whatever the topic might be, and then begin the first sentence with substantive information.

- If you are making several points or covering several topics, make a list and rank them in importance. Be sure the most important ones are mentioned near the top.

Asking for Permission

- I would like to
- I would appreciate the opportunity to
- Would it be acceptable to you if
- Is it possible that I could attend
- May I have your permission to
- I would like permission to quote two sentences from your book in the article I am writing.
- I am interested in
- I am planning to
- This is important because
- This will be of great benefit.
- This will have considerable impact.
- The reason this is significant is that
- Allowing me to do this will enable us to make important progress.
- A great learning opportunity
- Will make the process more efficient
- Will improve morale
- This will not affect
- Consistent with my performance goals
- In keeping with our discussion of …, I would like to
- Please keep in mind
- Will help us achieve our objective/goal
- I realize this is a significant request

Tips

- Be courteous and respectful; do not write with an air of entitlement.
- Spell out exactly what you want permission to do and why.

➡

- Say what the expected outcome is and how others might benefit, if that is known.
- Do not ingratiate yourself to the reader in an effort to get permission. It will sound phony and amateurish.

Proposing an Idea

- I have an idea I hope you will consider.
- Would increase productivity/efficiency/effectiveness
- This would enable us to
- In my experience, this has been beneficial.
- I think this can work as long as
- Better informed and better trained
- Will benefit the company by
- Timely
- Minimal cost
- At a substantial savings
- I am confident that
- You might want to consider
- This is a more practical and less expensive alternative.
- One option might be to
- This will have a significant long-term benefit.
- We stand to benefit in a big way.
- Although people have mentioned … , that is not a viable option. Instead, I propose
- Can we discuss the possibility of
- Would you consider
- There are a few reasons why I think this is feasible.
- Perhaps we should look at
- We tried …, and that failed. Then we tried …, and that did not work either.
- This will enable us to achieve our goal of
- If you are concerned about …, then we can
- At least a short-term solution
- I appreciate your consideration and look forward to hearing from you.

Tips

- Do not take long to state your idea. If the reader is supportive or neutral, you can propose your idea in the first paragraph. If the reader will be skeptical, ease in to your position by starting with information that will make your idea appealing.

- Sound confident. Avoid phrases such as "I think," "It seems to me that maybe," and "I'm not sure that this will work, but perhaps we might consider …" These give the impression that you are not sure of yourself.

- Have a collaborative tone. Sounding brazen might alienate the reader, and it might cause the reader to pay more attention to the tone than to your idea.

- Be sure your information unfolds logically from one element to the next. Great ideas can be lost on the reader when the information is disorganized.

Recommending a Course of Action

- The vice president asked us for our recommendation regarding
- I recommend/suggest that we
- If we sidestep the issue
- We cannot commit ourselves to … because
- We need to be careful about
- Given what we know
- Because of recent events
- Is the most practical answer
- Makes the most sense
- It is essential that we be involved, and here is why.
- This is a sensitive issue for
- From what we know
- Our understanding is that
- My concern/fear is that
- Our/her response should be
- One alternative might be that
- We should invest the effort
- We need to commit the necessary resources (people, time, money).
- It is difficult to imagine.
- I realize what this will mean
- I know that this course of action would create other issues.
- Will underscore our commitment to
- This will demonstrate our support for
- Will convey the impression that
- I am open to other ideas.
- Let's discuss this further.
- Please let me know what you think.

Tips

- Write with conviction, but do not be demanding or rash. Present your recommendation as a carefully considered idea.
- Explain why you are recommending this course of action.
- Make it clear, when appropriate, that you have considered different views and alternative suggestions.

Chapter 5

News Releases

The news release continues to be the standard written vehicle for reporting corporate news to the media, whether in the traditional format or purely as an e-mail communication.

The release should be about a news announcement—a new product, an event, or a fresh development in an ongoing story—and it should stay focused on news. It is not a marketing brochure.

It is written in the same format as that of most front-page newspaper articles. Begin with a one- or two-sentence snapshot of the news and the reason it is important, followed by supporting information that develops the news point. It is not necessary to begin with "The Cleaning Company today announced a new … " It is better to start with the news: "A new whirlygig that will wash and wax your floor while you are at the office was introduced today by the Cleaning Company."

Do not pack too much information into the first paragraph. Be selective about the traditional *who, what, where, when, why,* and *how.* Cramming all of them into the lead will create a bloated chunk of black text, which will deter the reader from continuing.

Choose which elements are most important. A news release not only must be newsworthy; it also must be visually inviting.

Keep the release to two pages, preferably one, particularly if it is for a Web site. That is a sufficient length to tell the news. If you want to provide additional information, provide links, Web sites, and other locations where the reader can find the material.

Announcing a Merger

- Has acquired/is merging with
- The new company will
- Under this new alliance
- Will enable us to expand/increase
- The intent is to create
- Will make us more competitive
- The acquisition will be accretive to earnings.
- Has merged in a stock-for-stock transaction
- The company has operations in
- Is a natural extension of our operations
- Has a reputation for high-quality products
- Is likely to lead to
- Will create new opportunities
- This represents an important step in the process of
- Has a record of successfully addressing challenges
- Our continuing effort to cut costs and improve the way we work
- We must make the right decisions to compete.
- This reinforces our long-held strategy to
- Improved economies of scale
- An excellent strategic fit
- Represents an outstanding opportunity to
- The merger is subject to approval by
- Company X brings to the new venture years of experience in

Tips

- Use a one-line headline, two lines if necessary, and use both uppercase and lowercase letters, but do not use all uppercase letters. It is difficult to read.

- Use a secondary headline, known as a subhead, only if there is something significant that is not covered in the headline. Subheads in news releases usually contribute little, and the added black text simply clutters the top of the page. Subheads are useful in some releases, but the reader usually goes immediately to the first paragraph to determine the news value.
- After capturing the essence of the news in the opening paragraph, proceed in an order of most-to-least importance. The second and third paragraphs should contain solid supporting information that expands on the lead.
- Background information, often called the "boilerplate," should appear at the end. This is general information describing the company, such as what it does or what it makes, where its locations are, how many employees it has, when it started in business. If a piece of background information is particularly significant, find a way to weave it in high in the release. But other background material should stay at the end.

New Business Model Announcement

- Is introducing
- According to the latest data
- The research shows
- The statistics are striking.
- The results suggest/indicate
- The intent is to create
- Under a new alliance with
- With this new product, the company will
- No longer will consumers/customers have to
- Will enable consumers and businesses to
- This partnership brings together the
- Improve efficiency
- Increase productivity
- Has received a major contract
- The first company to adopt
- The most advanced version
- Our commitment to reliable
- We see the need to invest in
- A tradition of high-quality products/services
- Energy efficient
- We are exploring
- We considered several options before deciding
- The study was conducted by
- These changes will improve the performance.
- The purpose of the campaign is to

Tips

- The headline should serve the same role as a newspaper headline, capturing the essence of the material underneath. It usually is not a complete thought. Make it one ➡

line, possibly two, and use strong verbs.

- The opening paragraph of the release, called the lead, should summarize the key elements of the news. The first sentence should contain the core news and a piece of information that tells why this product announcement is significant.

- Stay focused on the news. Do not issue a release laden with self-serving marketing messages. It is not a marketing document; it is a news release.

- Avoid the trite buzzwords that accompany so many new-product announcements. Words such as *unique, leverage, synergy, solution*, and *leading provider of* not only are tired and stale from overuse but also are vague, and frequently they are inaccurate. The reader, usually a journalist, takes great care to avoid using such words.

- It is not mandatory to have a quote from an executive discussing the announcement of a new product, but it is common. The quote usually appears in the third or fourth paragraph, though it can be inserted further down. Make it substantive. The quote should capture the speaker's expertise, insight, or sharp opinion. Avoid the universal "We are excited" quote; it is boring, it adds nothing, and journalists will not use it.

New Product Announcement

- Consumers/users will be able to
- Now will have access to
- The company says
- Extending its product line
- Reflects the company's move into a new market
- Consumers/businesses are demanding more.
- The first to achieve
- The first company to offer
- This is the first/only product of its kind.
- The most widely recognized name
- What makes this different is that
- Is based on the concept that
- Represents a significant advancement
- Has several new features
- Stronger capability
- Will improve productivity
- Enables a company to operate more efficiently
- Will see significant cost savings
- What distinguishes this is
- Includes several improvements
- Higher performance
- The product enables the user/customer to
- The ability to … represents a major advance.
- Rapidly growing
- Sophisticated equipment
- Is designed to be used to
- Company X manufactures

Tips

- Use a simple headline that is one line, two if necessary. ➡

It needs a verb and should capture the essence of the story, just as a newspaper headline does.

- The opening paragraph of the release, called the lead, should summarize the key elements of the news. The first sentence should contain the core news and a piece of information that tells why this announcement is significant.

- Avoid the trite buzzwords that accompany so many new-product announcements. Words such as *unique, leverage, synergy, solution,* and *leading provider of* not only are tired and stale from overuse but also are vague, and frequently they are inaccurate. The reader, usually a journalist, takes great care to avoid using such words.

- It is not mandatory to have a quote from an executive discussing the announcement, but it is common. The quote usually appears in the third or fourth paragraph, though it can be inserted further down. Make it substantive. The quote should capture the speaker's expertise, insight, or sharp opinion. Avoid the universal "We are excited" quote; it is boring, it adds nothing, and journalists will not use it.

New Appointment

- Is the new vice president of
- Will be responsible for
- In her new role, she will
- Will oversee/develop/implement
- Please join me in welcoming
- Prior to joining XYZ Corp., Mike spent 25 years at
- For more than 12 years, she has led
- She also served as vice president of HR at
- His vast knowledge of
- Brings an acute understanding of
- Brings more than 25 years of experience in
- Has held numerous positions in the marketing field
- As part of our strategy to
- This appointment reflects our commitment to
- We have created a new position to oversee
- Will focus on improving our

Tips

- Use a one-line headline, two lines if necessary, and use both uppercase and lowercase letters, but do not use all uppercase letters. It is difficult to read.
- Use a secondary headline, called a subhead, only if there is something significant that is not covered in the headline. Subheads in news releases usually contribute little, and the added black text simply clutters the top of the page. Subheads are useful in some releases, but the reader usually goes immediately to the first paragraph to determine the news value and pays little attention to subheads.
- After capturing the essence of the news in the opening paragraph, proceed in an order of most-to-least

➡

importance. The second and third paragraphs should contain solid supporting information that expands on the lead.

- Put background information about the company at the end of the news release.

Announcing Earnings

- Results showed a 7 percent gain in earnings for the quarter that ended June 30.
- Revenue was … compared with … in the same quarter last year.
- Diluted earnings per share were
- Comparable store sales were
- Net sales in the first quarter increased 15 percent, driven by strong growth in
- The results largely reflect strong contributions by the company's two new divisions.
- Candy Corp.'s fourth-quarter earnings per share (EPS) rose 17 percent.
- The company also continues to forecast that net cash from operating activities will be approximately
- These results/projections reflect continued strength in our real estate business.
- The results were within the guidance communicated in July.
- Predicts that equipment sales will decline/increase
- Is reducing production, which will allow the company to improve its cash position
- Were in line with
- In accordance with generally accepted accounting principles (GAAP)
- Net income for the quarter was
- We attribute the decline to
- That was offset by an increase in
- But that was balanced by
- Results for the year are still expected to be within the guidance communicated in July.

➡

- Because of shrinking demand in this sector of the industry
- Operating margins in the quarter increased to 20 percent, compared with 19 percent in the same quarter a year ago.

Tips

- The numbers appearing in the opening paragraph of an earnings release should be presented as GAAP results; that is, they are consistent with generally accepted accounting principles. GAAP is the standard that the Securities and Exchange Commission set to ensure that investors get a candid picture of how well a company is performing.
- Simplify the lead by focusing on one measurement of financial performance (you can choose which one). Avoid cramming too much information into the first paragraph, a common flaw in earnings releases.
- Any earnings release is likely to be laden with numbers, but do not smother the reader in digits. Use one or two numbers per sentence, and put them in context whenever it is appropriate so that the reader can make sense of them. Make comparisons to similar situations or familiar concepts, weave in explanation, and insert examples.

Chapter 6

E-mail

A List of Do's and Don'ts

Some people are under the illusion that they do not write memos; they only write e-mail, as if memos "really matter" and e-mail does not. They have the impression that you can write anything they want in an e-mail. But in the professional world, this is not the case. No longer is e-mail purely an "anything goes" chat line where readers casually tolerate mangled sentence structure, fragmented thoughts, erratic punctuation, and strikingly incorrect grammar.

In a quick one- or two-sentence note about meeting for lunch, most readers will not hold a writer to high standards. But because e-mail is the primary vehicle for communicating in business, many messages are about substantive issues pertaining to daily corporate business. Readers, particularly in management, do not have the patience to undertake an "investigation," searching for clues in the text and making additional phone calls to clarify your meaning.

Start with a specific subject line. Do not use one or two words that are so vague that they tell the reader nothing about what is in the note of importance. Use 9 or 10 words if necessary. Then craft a tightly written message that conveys the most important information in the first paragraph. Think about what questions the reader might have, and be sure to answer those in the body.

If appropriate, include a few details from the previous message, so that the reader has a frame of reference as he or she reads your message. Be careful about using pronouns, such as *he, she, they, it*, that might relate ambiguously to a person or thing in an earlier communication. You know what or whom you are referring to, but the reader might not.

Remember that every e-mail message has your name on it, so take pride in your writing. Read through it before hitting the "send" button, and remember that your goal is to communicate a message that the reader can comprehend quickly.

Announcing a New Program

- This will provide a terrific opportunity to
- We hope this new program will enable you to
- Our goal is to
- As of June 1,
- Please see the attachment for details.
- For a few years, people have asked about the possibility
- The purpose of the program is to
- You will receive enrollment materials beginning
- The program will allow people to
- We hope that you will participate.
- The new program will provide several benefits, including
- The leadership development program is open to all managers.
- To participate, go the intranet and click on
- To participate in the program, you need to
- People who enroll will
- As a participant, your commitment is to
- There is no requirement.
- The program underscores our commitment to
- Demonstrates/signifies the importance we attach to

Tips

- Highlight the benefits to the reader.
- Say what led to the creation of the program.
- Provide all the details needed to sign up, and provide a contact name and number.

E-mail Complaint

- I realize that there might be extenuating circumstances.
- I understand how this might happen.
- I would appreciate it if you could look into this.
- Please let me know if there is any information I can provide.
- We all are under pressure, and I think it is reasonable to expect
- I realize that this might be an oversight on this end.
- Please check to see if
- Perhaps if we work together, we can prevent this from happening again.
- Our standard practice is to …, and that is not being followed.
- I understood that to mean …, and that is not what happened.
- It has been (length of time), and I have not heard anything so I thought I would follow up.
- It is my fault that we did not meet the deadline. I will be more vigilant next time.
- I would appreciate it if you could
- It is difficult, given all that we are juggling already, to have to monitor
- Thanks very much for your help.

Tips

- Because e-mail is so convenient, people often write messages when they are not in the right state of mind. Avoid writing a complaint note when you are still annoyed. The message must have a calm, professional tone to be effective.

- Do not be accusatory and do not be harshly critical. There might be circumstances you are not aware of, and even if you are right, no reader wants to be humiliated.
- The more respectful and positive you are, the more likely you are to get the results you want.

E-mail Policy Announcements

- Under the new policy, employees will
- Here are the major changes
- To help people through the transition
- As everyone becomes more familiar with the policy
- This will mark a significant step forward.
- In the interests of maintaining high expectations
- The policy is necessary because
- Please read the policy carefully and pay special attention to
- We asked for your input, and we heard you
- We are committed to managing all our operations in a manner that
- This is why we have developed this new policy.
- In the past, our policy has been to ... but we recognize the need to go further.
- As part of our plan/effort to ... we want to put in place a policy that will
- This policy should cause minimal inconvenience.
- If you have questions, please call or send an e-mail to
- Rising costs/changes in the market have forced us to
- Here is what will not change.
- The most significant elements of the policy are

Tips

- Explain clearly what the policy is, what the impact will be, and what the expectations are.
- Say why the new policy or changes are necessary and emphasize any direct benefits.
- Provide contact information for anyone with the knowledge and authority to answer questions.

Routine Response Providing Information

- The information you sent is great.
- I will call you next week.
- The person you want to speak with is
- I'm sorry that you had trouble; I don't know why that happened.
- If you want additional information, please go to our Web site.
- You asked for contact information for Lori. You can reach her at
- Attached is a PDF file that explains
- Great to hear from you.
- Thank you for your inquiry.
- Sorry that I'm just getting back to you.
- Thanks for your message.
- Below are suggestions for
- If you need more, let me know.
- This has several advantages.
- A couple of quick thoughts

Tips

- The reader should know within the first couple of sentences what the point of your message is and why he or she needs to deal with it. If the message is four paragraphs or longer, start with a summary paragraph to capture the critical information the reader needs.
- If you plan to discuss several points, tell the reader that in the opening paragraph, so that the reader continues to read. When reading e-mail, people are eager to hit the delete button, and they will unless they know there is a reason to continue reading.
- Be sure to include all the information the reader needs.

Asking Reader to Do Something

- Can you do me a favor and find out?
- Will you check to see if
- Please clarify.
- I have a couple of questions.
- I hope you can help.
- Your help will be appreciated.
- Thanks very much.
- I appreciate your help.
- I know you're busy, but I'm in a bind.
- I am doing some research into ... and would appreciate your insight.
- Tell me what you think.
- I will take care of ... if you can handle
- Two reasons why this is important:
- You have the knowledge and experience to
- Would you be willing to

Tips

- Given the volume of e-mail that people must plow through, be clear about your request, and if there is a deadline, present it quickly.
- If you expect that this will be inconvenient for the reader, explain why you need to impose on him or her.
- Dates, times, and places must be accurate.

Proposing an Idea

- Tell me what you think of this idea.
- I might have an option that would be more effective.
- What about those people who
- Is it really necessary to
- I think this can work as long as
- This will address a few problems:
- What do you think about
- We will be a better department.
- Will benefit the company by
- I think the timing is right.
- Given the alternatives, the cost is reasonable.
- This will save us money in the long term.
- What do you think the objections will be if
- I appreciate your consideration and look forward to hearing from you.

Tips

- If you expect that your reader will be supportive, or will at least listen to your idea, present it quickly. If the reader needs to be convinced, you can use an inductive pattern, in which you state a few facts and lead the reader to the conclusion you want him or her to make.
- Write with confidence and conviction. Avoid hedging language, such as, "It seems to me that maybe" or "I'm not sure that this will work, but …"
- Have a collaborative tone. Be open to other ideas.

Conveying Disappointing News

- You invested considerable effort, and I appreciate that.
- This means/does not mean
- I expect that there will be additional opportunities.
- You can make a significant contribution by
- Although it might not work this year, it is a good idea.
- Your commitment was significant, and I appreciate the effort.
- You are an asset to our department.
- In reaching this decision, I considered
- Having said that, we still can
- After examining all the details, I realized that I could not
- Can you suggest the next step?
- Please let me know if you have other ideas.
- Here are a couple of suggestions to improve your proposal/chances for approval.
- One factor that you might consider
- The encouraging news is

Tips

- Be tactfully direct; do not be vague.
- Ease into the negative news by starting with a positive or neutral statement that the reader cannot argue with. Convey the disappointing news and exit with a positive tone.
- Express your disappointment in not being able to deliver positive news and try to be helpful.

Appendices

Key Business Writing Skills

Appendices

Appendix One

Writing with Clarity

No quality of business communication is more in demand than clarity. Throughout corporate America, people bemoan the muddled writing found in routine messages, formal documents, newsletter articles, and letters to customers. Newspaper headlines provide biting reminders: "What Corporate America Can't Build: A Sentence" and "Buzzword Backlash Looks to Purge Jibba-Jabba out of Corporate-Speak." Poor organization, contorted sentence structure, imprecise word choice, and length combine to cost companies millions of dollars in wasted time as employees are forced to decipher and rewrite messages that were poorly written the first time.

To help a reader breeze through your writing, try these tips:

- **Choose the appropriate format.** Not all information you write should fit into the same organizational structure. Most information should be presented in a most-to-least important order, starting with a summary paragraph that captures the essential pieces of information the reader must know. Details will follow further down.

- **Keep paragraphs in readable chunks.** Focus on one topic per paragraph, link sentences so there is a cohesive flow from one idea to the next, and limit most paragraphs to two to four sentences or five lines of text. Long paragraphs are difficult for a reader to handle. Consider using a topic sentence at the beginning to capture the theme of the paragraph. It is not mandatory, but it can help the reader.

- **Crafting the clear, direct sentence.** Sentence structures and lengths will vary, but build most sentences around the key elements: the subject, verb, and object (when the verb has an object). A reader cannot understand a sentence without knowing the subject and verb, so if you position them near the front of the sentence, the reader can quickly grasp the meaning of the sentence. Most sentences should be in the range of 12 to 20 words, but some will be longer, some shorter.

- **Know when to use the passive voice.** Although the active construction is more direct and less wordy, the passive structure is sometimes more appropriate. Consider these two sentences:

  > We have a new benefits policy. It was approved yesterday by the CEO.

It is a pronoun representing *policy*. Positioning *It* early in the second sentence provides a sense of continuity and enables the reader to relate the second sentence to the first. Making the second sentence active by starting with *The CEO* would not provide that cohesion. Logically connecting the sentences in this way is more important than making every sentence active.

■ **Do not let strong verbs become buried in nouns.** Words that end in *ent, ence, ance,* or *ing* usually function as nouns, and they often contain action that should serve as the verb in the sentence.

NO: We have completed a review of the plan.

YES: We reviewed the plan. (*reviewed* is stronger than *have completed*.)

NO: We made significant improvements in customer service.

YES: We improved customer service significantly.

■ **Trim the flab.** Remove words that contribute nothing to your meaning.

NO: on a monthly basis; various kinds of projects; in the near future

YES: monthly; projects; soon

■ **Be wary of adjectives and adverbs.** Pay special attention to words ending in *ly*. Either drop the modifier or replace the modifier and the noun with a stronger word.

NO: really upset; highly unusual; ultimate goal

YES: angry; rare; goal

- **Write with specifics.** Using buzzwords is a sign of lazy writing. Rather than reach for the same stale words and phrases, choose a word that is more familiar and more specific. Help the reader "see."

  NO: initiative; functionality

  YES: program, plan, project, goal, tactic, campaign; capability or features

- **Turn phrases into single-word modifiers.** One way to improve efficiency is to reduce prepositional phrases to single adjectives.

  NO: We have a directive from management to consider the opinions of employees.

  YES: We have a management directive to consider employees' opinions.

- **Avoid stockpiling modifiers in front of another word.** It creates an awkward sentence.

  NO: The Defense document security service marking guide

  YES: A guide to marking classified Defense documents

  TIP: The way to avoid such a construction is usually to take the noun at the end (*guide*) and move it closer to the front of the sentence and put the descriptive words after it.

- **Avoid long introductory elements that march ahead of the subject and verb.** The longer the reader must wait to see the subject and verb, the more likely he or she is to skim the beginning to hurry and locate the main idea.

NO: Recognized worldwide by the advertising industry for his creative influence on the Chrysler Corporation's successful brand advertising, and for his vision behind the most creative commercials in the world, Gary Topolewski earned the award.

YES: Gary Topolewski earned the award. He has been recognized worldwide by the advertising industry….

TIP: The main idea of the sentence is contained in the main clause *Gary Topolewski earned the award*. Moving it to the front of the paragraph and making it a separate sentence is one way to recast the sentence.

■ Do not put too many words between the subject and the verb.

NO: The *report* about the company study that was done to determine the relationship of dollars spent on employee education to improved performance *is summarized* below.

YES: This *report summarizes* the study that was done to determine….

TIP: A reader needs to know both the subject and verb to know what is happening in the sentence. The reader of the original sentence would see report and then race past the information in the middle, eager to find out what the report is doing. Then the reader would have to go back and reread the sentence.

Appendix Two

Observe Your Tone

Many messages fail to communicate not because the information is unclear but because the reader is paying more attention to the tone than to the message itself. An abrasive tone becomes a distraction.

Here are a few suggestions:

- **Be tactful.** Empathize with the reader; we all are human and capable of embarrassing blunders. If you need to be firm, you can be, but do not be harshly critical or sarcastic.
- **Be candid.** People appreciate honesty and sincerity, particularly from managers. Do not be afraid to apologize.
- **Use *you* and *your*** in routine or positive messages but stick with *I* or *we* statements as much as possible when the situation involves discipline or a disagreement.
- **Be constructive.** The more positive you are, the more likely you are to get the results you want. A person reading your message is seeing and hearing your personality in the text. What kind of impression do you want to leave with the reader?

- **Choose your words carefully.** People interpret words differently. A word or phrase that you think is harmless might have a different connotation to the reader. Such words as *failed, neglected to, sloppy, careless,* and *how could you?* are inflammatory.

Appendix Three

Establishing the Right Style

For decades, business letters and memos were written in a stilted style because, we assumed, a corporate message had to sound "businesslike." Although such formality was once considered proper, it is now frowned upon as cold, distant, and pompous.

You do not need two distinct writing styles, one that you would use on the telephone and one you would use on paper. Naturally, a face-to-face or telephone conversation usually will be less structured and more relaxed because it is a spontaneous give and take. But with a little polish here and there to ensure correct grammar and punctuation, you can have a writing style that is professionally conversational and will serve most audiences.

Here are a few things to keep in mind:

- **Conversational writing sounds natural.** Your sentences should sound the way they would if you talked to the person in the hall or on the phone. When you use stilted phrases that you probably would not use in a conversation, you sound stuffy and artificial.

- **Be careful about wanting to "make an impression."**
  Often, the reader's impression is that the writer went out
  of his way to sound impressive and instead sounds phony.

- **Avoid stilted phrases that are obsolete.** They put
  distance between you and the reader. If the sentence says
  "Please be advised that the meeting has been postponed,"
  simply say, "The meeting has been postponed." You are
  not giving advice. "Enclosed please find" can be replaced
  by "Enclosed is," "Here is," or "Attached is," and the phrase
  "Per your request" is probably not something you would
  ever say to another person in a conversation, so there is
  no need to open a written message with it.

- **Exit gracefully and quickly. Avoid endings that do not
  contain useful information.** "I hope this information is
  helpful. If I can be of further assistance or if I can answer
  any questions, please don't hesitate to call me at your
  convenience." If you answer questions, you are being of
  further assistance, so that is redundant. When you need
  to call someone about something, do you check their last
  message to see if it says "don't hesitate to call"? When
  people want your attention, they will call you, regardless
  of what your message said, and they will not call you when
  it is inconvenient for them, so it is not necessary to say
  "at your convenience." All that is necessary in a closing line
  is something simple, such as, "Call or write anytime if you
  have questions."

Common Grammatical Flaws

■ **Subject-verb agreement.** The subject must agree with the verb in number (singular with singular, plural with plural).

EXAMPLE: The variety of seminars and courses available often confuse people.

SOLUTION: Add an *s* to **confuse** to make it singular so that it agrees with **variety**.

■ **Proper form of pronouns.** Present pronouns in the subjective form when they function as subjects; use the objective form when they serve as objects.

EXAMPLE: This is a frequent topic of discussion among Kathy, John, and I.

SOLUTION: Change *I* to *me*, which is the objective form. The pronoun is functioning as the object of the preposition *among*. The pronoun can only serve as a subject or an object and must appear in the form that is appropriate to that role.

■ **Parallelism.** When you have a series of elements in a sentence (two or more), present them as the same part of speech. The similarity of form shows the reader that the elements are related, and the consistency makes the information easier to read.

EXAMPLE: Employees need to know **what our philosophy is**, our **goals**, and **we appreciate their work**. (clause + noun + complete sentence)

SOLUTION: Employees need to know our **philosophy**, our **goals**, and our **appreciation** of their work. (noun + noun + noun)

OR: Employees need to know **what our philosophy is**, **what our goals are**, and **that we appreciate their work**. (clause + clause + clause)

■ **Misplaced and dangling modifiers.** Keep modifiers close to the words they describe or refer to.

Misplaced

EXAMPLE: The computers contain information on customers and products **that can help you**.

SOLUTION: Move the modifying clause *that can help you* closer to *information*, which is what it is referring to.

BETTER: The computer contains information **that can help you** learn about customers and products.

Dangling

EXAMPLE: Since becoming a manager, the feedback process has been part of my job.

SOLUTION: *becoming* is a verb form that refers to someone becoming, but that person is not in the sentence. The complete modifier, *Since becoming a manager*, hangs there because it does not logically link to anything in the sentence. The person or thing that the modifier refers to must appear soon after the comma.

BETTER: Since becoming a manager, *I* have been involved in the feedback process.

■ **Proper verb tense.** Verb tense expresses time. Use the appropriate tense to show when things occurred. The three main tenses are *past*, *present*, and *future*, but we also have the *perfect* tenses.

EXAMPLE: I noticed that the new manufacturing operation was moved across town.

SOLUTION: The sentence has two verbs, *noticed,* and *was moved,* which tells the reader that the "noticing" and the "moving" happened at the same time. But they did not; the moving had occurred earlier. When two things happened in the past and one happened earlier than the other, **use the past perfect tense, which requires** *had*

BETTER: I noticed that the new manufacturing operation **had** moved across town.

Common Myths about Grammar

■ **Never start a sentence with *because* or *however*.** *Because* is a conjunction (*because of* is a compound preposition) and *however* is an adverb. Good writers have started sentences with them for centuries. If you begin with *because,* just be careful not to make that introductory piece too long.

> ***Because*** *both departments are involved, you need to plan carefully.*

> *It was a great entry.* ***However****, we missed the deadline.*

■ **Never end a sentence with a preposition.** It is considered acceptable, and great writers have done it for 200 years.

This "rule" appears to have been an arbitrary preference of rigid constructionists who wanted English to resemble Latin and Germanic languages, from which English was evolving. In Latin, a preposition always precedes a noun; it never appears as the final word in a sentence.

> *Here is the information you were looking for* is more natural than *Here is the information for which you were looking.*

- **Do not split infinitives.** (Infinitives are verb forms in which a main verb is usually accompanied by *to*.) Do not do it carelessly, but good writers have split infinitives for 200 years because sometimes that is the most effective way to add emphasis to a verb.

> *I need you **to** really **understand** the importance of this.*

- **Never start a sentence with *and*.** Starting with *and* helps the reader connect the thought to the one in the previous sentence, thus providing a smooth transition between ideas. It avoids an abrupt beginning of a sentence. Use it sparingly, but it is acceptable today.

> *We need to do A, B, C, and D. And that's not all. We also ... .*

- **Never use sentence fragments.** Always write in complete sentences. Fragments are sometimes used for effect. Business communication is more polished than conversation, but occasional fragments help create a breezy, conversational tone and they help to add emphasis.

For years, people have assumed this practice is wrong.
Not quite.

Commonly Confused Words

■ **affect/effect**

affect, verb: to have an impact or an influence on something.

> *The changes affected our department.*
> (This is the most common usage.)

affect, noun: a feeling or emotion.

effect, noun: a result, an impact; the power to produce a result.

> *She had a significant effect on our staff.*

> *The medication had an immediate effect on him.*

effect, verb: to cause or to bring about.

> *The new manager wants to effect change from the status quo.*

■ **principle/principal**

principle, noun: a truth, an assumption, a standard of good behavior.

> *He is a man of principle.*

principal, noun: the highest or most important in rank.

> *That is his principal concern.*

■ **assure/ensure**

assure, verb: to inform positively; to remove doubt; to give confidence to.

She assured him that he would get there on time.

ensure, verb: to make certain.

TIP: *assure* refers to people.

■ **farther/further**

farther, adv.: to or at a more distant, remote point.

I plan to hike farther up the trail this year.

further, adj.: More distant in degree, time, or space.

The candidate moved further to the right.

further, adv.: to a greater extent.

We can discuss this further after the meeting.

TIP: In recent years, *farther* has been restricted to physical distance.

■ **less/fewer**

less, adj.: not as great in amount or quantity.

I would like to spend less time in the car.

less, adv.: a smaller extent.

She is less enthusiastic.

few, adj.: consisting of a small number.

I need a few groceries.

TIP: *Fewer* is applied to things you can count. *Less* is used to describe measurable amounts: less sand, less than a bushel of berries.

- **infer/imply**

  infer, verb: to conclude from evidence; to reason from circumstance.

  I inferred from her speech that major changes are pending.

  imply, verb: to express indirectly; to suggest.

  I didn't mean to imply that you were wrong.

- **allusion/illusion**

  allusion, noun: an indirect reference.

  His speech contained an allusion to poor management.

  illusion, noun: an erroneous perception of reality.

  He is under the illusion that writing is not important.

- **continual/continuous**

  continual, adj.: recurring regularly or frequently, usually at intervals.

  I continually remind him to pay the insurance premium.

  continuous, adj.: uninterrupted in time or sequence.

  The ocean tide moves continuously in and out.

■ **all ready/already**

all ready: everyone is prepared.

> *We are all ready to go.*

already, adv.: by this time or before a specified time.

> *The children are already packed.*

■ **a while/awhile**

awhile, adv.: for a short time.

> *I only can stay awhile.*

while, noun: a period of time.

> *He has worked there for a while.*

TIP: *Awhile* is never preceded by a preposition, only by a verb: I need to rest awhile. The phrase *a while* is preceded by a preposition. *The car will be in the shop for a while.*

■ **comprise/compose**

comprise, verb: to consist of, to be composed of.

> *Our committee comprises a range of viewpoints.*

compose, verb: to form by combining elements, to make up the parts of.

> *Many states compose our country.*

> *Mud is composed of dirt and water.*

■ **stationary/stationery**

stationary, adj.: not movable, in a fixed position.

For exercise, I ride the stationary bike.

stationery, noun: writing paper and envelopes.

■ **compliment/complement**

compliment, noun: an expression of praise or admiration.

She complimented him on his behavior.

complement, noun: something that completes a whole or brings to perfection; either of two parts that complete each other.

She complemented the other players on her team.

The two women ran the department together because they complemented each other so well.

About the Author

Ken O'Quinn, principal of *Writing with Clarity*, is a professional writing coach who conducts workshops and one-on-one coaching in corporations and in global public relations firms. He spent 21 years in daily journalism, including 12 years with the Associated Press, before becoming a writing coach.

He teaches business writing, managerial communication, and journalistic writing for corporate communications and public relations professionals. He also is a writing instructor for the National Investor Relations Institute.

He has worked with such companies as Chevron, Oracle, Intel, Visa, Eli Lilly, Campbell Soup, Morgan Stanley, Fidelity Investments, Motorola, Raytheon, Sprint, Reebok, Blockbuster, 7-11, Merck, and with such public relations clients as Edelman, Ogilvy, Porter Novelli, Fleishman Hillard, PR Newswire, and Burson-Marsteller.

Ken also has been a guest speaker at the IABC and PRSA international conferences. He is based in Cape Elizabeth, Maine.

Ken's Web site is www.WritingWithClarity.com.